SUCCESSFUL NEGOTIATION:
TRIESTE 1954

Successful Negotiation:
TRIESTE 1954

*An Appraisal by
the Five Participants*

EDITED BY JOHN C. CAMPBELL

PRINCETON UNIVERSITY PRESS

Copyright © 1976 by Princeton University Press
Published by Princeton University Press
Princeton and Guildford, Surrey

ALL RIGHTS RESERVED

Prepared under the auspices of
The Communications Institute under a grant from
The Schweppe Research and Education Fund

Library of Congress Cataloging in Publication Data
will be found on the last printed page of this book

Composed and printed in the United States of America
by Princeton University Press, Princeton, New Jersey

FOREWORD

This small volume is an unusual approach to an unusual case of negotiating.

The successful 1954 settlement of the long-standing dispute over Trieste was extraordinary in a number of ways—even more so when viewed in the perspective of twenty years. This book attempts not to present a detailed history, but rather to offer the unscreened and unadulterated recollections and evaluations of the five experienced and skilled men who conducted the negotiations. From these it also attempts to analyze the factors that might have wider applicability.

The project is part of the Communication and Conflict program carried on by the Communications Institute of the Academy for Educational Development. Those responsible concluded long ago that much could be learned from analysis of successful negotiations and from the recollections of successful negotiators. Joseph E. Johnson, senior consultant to the program, suggested that the unusual Trieste negotiations of 1954 provided a singular opportunity because, even after twenty years, the five principal negotiators were still alive and alert. John C. Campbell was enlisted to play a major hand in the project. His career had embraced not only knowledge of the Trieste dispute and settlement but also State Department experience and distinction as a scholar at the Council on Foreign Relations. He was asked to join Mr. Johnson in conducting the interviews and to under-

FOREWORD

take both the introduction and the conclusion to the volume.

As noted earlier, this book is not an exercise in detailed diplomatic history. This has been done, insofar as practicable without access to the American and British documents, in two studies by Jean-Baptiste Duroselle and Bogdan C. Novak. It will, presumably, be done again when historians gain access to all the documentation. This book was designed as something quite different from the conventional history or the conventional study by a single scholar. It is a specific study of a diplomatic success centering on the firsthand recollections and evaluations of all five principal negotiators. Mr. Campbell ably provides the scene-setting introduction and the final chapter of conclusions.

It is believed that this unusual approach, presented within relatively brief compass, will be of unique value to negotiators, future negotiators, and students of the negotiating process. If so, they will join us in gratitude to the five distinguished diplomats, to John C. Campbell and Joseph E. Johnson, to Maureen R. Berman for her general assistance, and to the Schweppe Research and Education Fund, which has made this program possible.

EDWARD W. BARRETT

Communications Institute
New York, New York

CONTENTS

FOREWORD	v
MAPS	
1. The "Julian March" Region	ix
2. The Free Territory of Trieste	x
INTRODUCTION. The Story in Brief	3
CHAPTER ONE. The American Negotiator, Llewellyn E. Thompson	23
CHAPTER TWO. The British Negotiator, Geoffrey W. Harrison	45
CHAPTER THREE. The Yugoslav Negotiator, Vladimir Velebit	76
CHAPTER FOUR. The Italian Negotiator, Manlio Brosio	110
CHAPTER FIVE. Catalyst of the Final Agreement, Robert D. Murphy	128
CONCLUSION. What is to be Learned?	145
APPENDICES	
A. Memorandum of Understanding between the Governments of Italy, the United Kingdom of Great Britain and Northern Ireland, the United States of America and Yugoslavia Regarding the Free Territory of Trieste	159
Annex II, Special Statute	162
B. Letter from President Eisenhower to Marshal Tito, delivered in Belgrade, Yugoslavia, by Ambassador Robert D. Murphy, September 1954	168

CONTENTS

C. Letter of Instructions from Acting Secretary of State W. B. Smith to Ambassador Thompson, January 28, 1954 — 170
D. Announcement of Agreement, Department of State Press Release 554, dated October 5, 1954 — 175

INDEX — 177

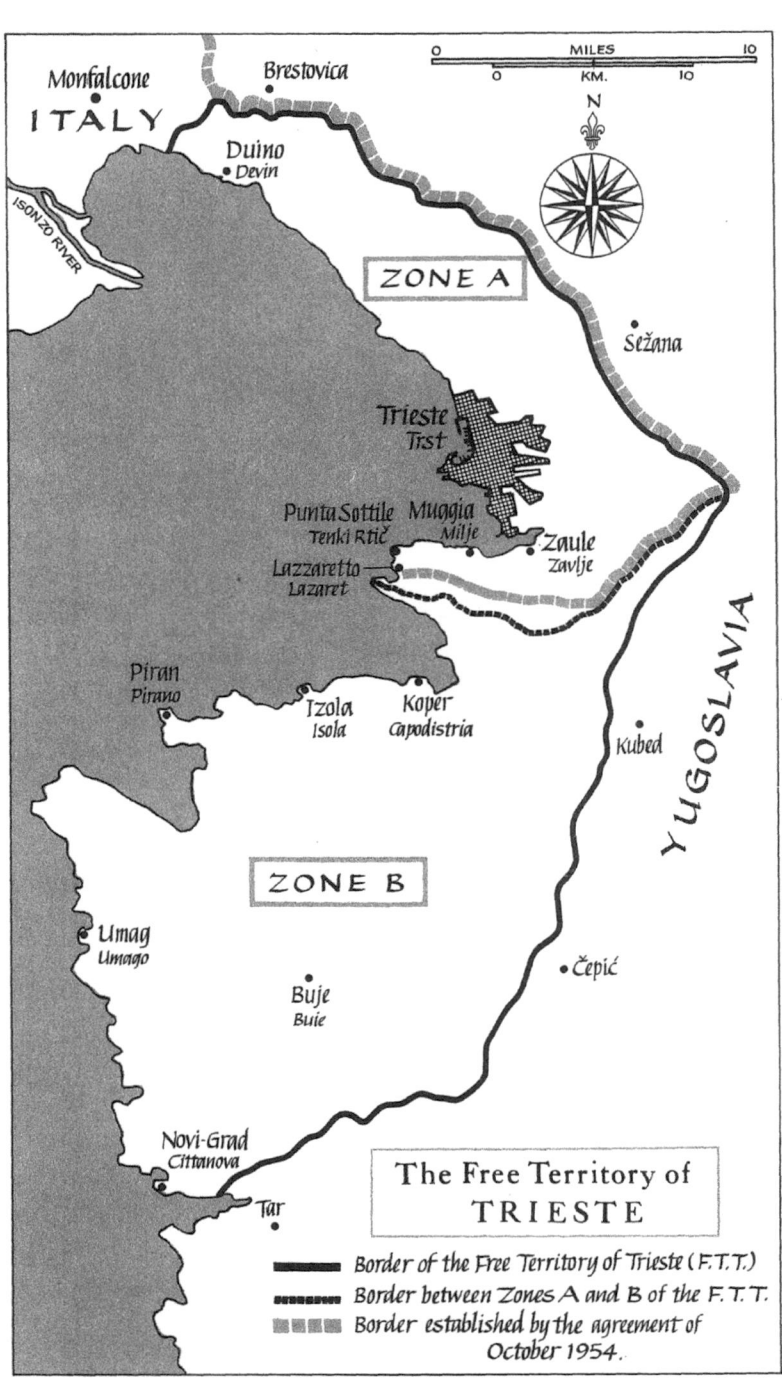

SUCCESSFUL NEGOTIATION:
TRIESTE 1954

INTRODUCTION

The Story in Brief

The problem of Trieste was one of the classic territorial disputes in European history. For years it defied solution by the contesting parties and by outside powers. Yet in 1954, a set of intensive secret negotiations suddenly produced an agreement that not only resolved the deadlock but ushered in a period of remarkably good relations between Italy and Yugoslavia. The polemics and the threat of military action disappeared, and the border in the Trieste area became a model of local cooperation, with large numbers of people crossing it legally and without hindrance every day for work or recreation.

The revival of public argument between the two governments in 1974 over the juridical finality of the border may be a salutary reminder that such territorial disputes cannot be permanently laid to rest as long as strong national feelings exist and governments are tempted to exploit them. In this case, however, the question of sovereignty had been deliberately avoided in the negotiations in order to make an agreement possible; and the Italian government never agreed that the "Memorandum of Understanding," which constituted the agreement, extinguished its claim to all territories on the other side of the border. But twenty years of acceptance on both sides have left their mark, and it does not seem likely that the settlement will be upset.

The negotiations of 1954 were aided by a number of diplomatic techniques; some were common, some out of

INTRODUCTION

the ordinary. Their net effect was to bring about a successful result that could hardly have been attained by other means. The interviews with the principal negotiators, which supply the main substance of this book, provide us with a unique picture of this exercise in diplomacy, combining firsthand testimony with reflective criticism from the perspective of two decades.

Each negotiator, in giving his own views, tells much of the story of the Trieste dispute in its final phase. But their accounts will be better understood if they are introduced by a brief historical survey of the dispute and previous failures to settle it, and by a statement of the highlights of the negotiations of 1954. This survey draws on the work of others who have written the history of the conflict, and on some key U.S. documents which the Department of State agreed on request to declassify.[1]

THE NATURE OF THE PROBLEM

The "Julian March," or Venezia Giulia, comprising Trieste, Istria, and other territories at the head of the Adriatic, was bitterly disputed between Italy and Yugoslavia from the time of World War I, when each sought to gain it from the ruins of the Austro-Hungarian Empire. The conflict and the depth of feeling on both sides do not date from 1918, however, but from cen-

[1] Two excellent comprehensive histories of the dispute are Jean-Baptiste Duroselle, *Le Conflit de Trieste 1943–1954* (Brussels: Institut de Sociologie de L'Université Libre de Bruxelles, 1966); and Bogdan C. Novak, *Trieste, 1941–1954: The Ethnic, Political, and Ideological Struggle* (Chicago and London: University of Chicago Press, 1970). There is also a major Yugoslav work by Janko Jeri, *Tržaško vprašanje po drugi svetovni vojni: Tri faze diplomatskega boja* (Ljubljana: Cankarjeva Založba, 1961). M. Duroselle's account profits from the access he was given to certain unpublished documents in the Italian and Yugoslav archives. I am indebted to Professor Novak for a number of suggestions on the manuscript.

THE STORY IN BRIEF

turies before, and are rooted in the differences between the Italians, heirs of the Roman and Venetian traditions, who naturally asserted themselves on the coasts of "their" Adriatic, and the South Slavs, who had peopled the hinterland and pushed down to the sea. These differences grew in intensity with the rise of nationalism in the nineteenth century.

To oversimplify a complex problem, by 1918 the ethnic map showed a line of division between Italians and Yugoslavs running roughly along the Isonzo (Soča) River, but to the east of that line were located a big Italian city with a substantial Slovene minority, Trieste (Trst), and several smaller coastal towns with Italian majorities. All were surrounded by a countryside populated by Slovenes and Croats, whose settlements at many points came all the way to the coast. The economic map showed a natural connection between the port of Trieste and its hinterland, a connection long recognized by Vienna, which had developed it into a flourishing port serving a large area of central Europe.

The peace settlement following World War I in this area was determined neither by ethnic factors nor by economics, but by politics. Italy had more political muscle behind its claims than did Yugoslavia, despite President Wilson's efforts to get a better deal for the latter. It is worth noting, however, that there was no dispute among the powers about Italy's acquisition of Trieste itself. The disputes were about where the frontier would run east of Trieste, and about Fiume (Rijeka). Italy won the disputes and acquired a large area of ethnically Yugoslav territory.[2]

[2] The relevant treaties were those between Italy and Yugoslavia signed at Rapallo (November 12, 1920), establishing the frontier and making Fiume an independent free state; and at Rome (January 27, 1924), recognizing the annexation of Fiume by Italy.

5

INTRODUCTION

The problem was settled in a legal sense, in that Yugoslavia ultimately signed the treaties that fixed the postwar frontiers. But it was not solved as a political problem because the Yugoslavs were not reconciled to the settlement, and because Mussolini's policy of persecution and denationalization of the Yugoslav minority in Italy further envenomed the issue. The events of World War II, in which Italy annexed some parts of Yugoslavia, occupied others, and supported the infamous Pavelić regime in Croatia, helped to harden the determination of the Yugoslavs at the close of the war to reverse the territorial decisions of 1920–1924 and gain Trieste once and for all.

Units of Tito's army entered the city at the end of April 1945, but were forced to withdraw when Allied troops came in two days later. In subsequent exchanges the British and American governments presented Tito with what amounted to an ultimatum. A line separating the zones of Allied and Yugoslav occupation of former Italian territory was established, and Allied troops took over control of Trieste.

This decision, which risked a military clash with Tito's forces, was taken by the Western Allies partly because of the need for Trieste as the essential supply point for their future zones of occupation in Austria; but, even more importantly, it was a logical effort to hold open the question of the territorial settlement and to save a large Italian city from *de facto* annexation by Yugoslavia. The U.S. acting Secretary of State, following the principle laid down by Roosevelt, announced that territorial disputes were to be resolved at the peace table and not by "armies on the march."[3] The fact that Italy had

---

3 *Department of State Bulletin*, May 13, 1945, p. 902. President Truman, meeting with his advisers on May 10, came to the conclusion that

by this time become a "co-belligerent" and had good relations with the Western powers and that the victorious partisan forces in Yugoslavia were led by communists were relevant factors. Winston Churchill did not fancy Trieste in Yugoslav (read: Russian) hands.

What seemed a reasonable if unpleasant decision to the Western powers appeared to the Yugoslavs an act of brute force, the betrayal of an ally who had fought hard and endured great sacrifices. It was difficult for the British and Americans to grasp the depth of the anger and bitterness on the Yugoslav side, anger felt not just by the communist-led regime—newly in power, with an assumed mandate to realize the historic rights of the peoples of Yugoslavia, and shaken in its prestige by such a setback—but also by the people, regardless of political persuasion. The Yugoslavs sensed a finality in this "provisional" decision, just as they had anticipated the finality of their own "liberation" of the city. The way in which they had lost Trieste, in addition to the fact of having lost it, colored their attitude toward a negotiated settlement for years to come. Many Yugoslavs were also convinced that Italy did not really want Trieste for itself, but only wanted to deny it to Yugoslavia and to use it against Yugoslav interests.

When the Council of Foreign Ministers met in London in September 1945 to draft a peace treaty for Italy, it was up against a situation in which the parties directly concerned had totally irreconcilable positions, feelings on both sides were inflamed, and the great powers had no agreed plan or purpose.

---

the only solution was to "throw them out," as Churchill was urging. See the diplomatic correspondence in *Foreign Relations of the United States, 1945*, 4 (Washington, D.C., Government Printing Office, 1968), 1103–1187; Winston S. Churchill, *The Second World War*, 6 (Boston: Houghton Mifflin, 1953), 551–561.

INTRODUCTION

THE PERIOD OF NONNEGOTIABILITY, *1945–1953*

There was a certain unreality in all the debates and negotiations over the disposition of Trieste in the peace settlement. Neither Italy nor Yugoslavia had a significant influence on the proceedings, which were in the hands of the big powers. The three Western Allies proposed three different lines, all of which left Trieste to Italy; the Soviet Union supported the Yugoslav claim to the city, and much more. A four-power commission of experts sent to the disputed area reached no agreement on recommendations for the location of the frontier because their governments were concerned with bigger things than the collection of facts and figures. The experts recommended four separate lines. In due course, in order to break the deadlock, all four powers compromised on a solution that established the "French line" as the boundary between Italy and Yugoslavia, except in the Trieste area, where the creation of a separate Free Territory of Trieste (F.T.T.) denied the city and some nearby districts to both contending parties. Neither was happy with it. The Yugoslavs, though getting virtually all the rest of the ethnically Yugoslav territory gained by Italy after World War I and some preponderantly Italian towns as well, remained unreconciled to the loss of Trieste. They felt that they had been sold out by the Russians as well as by the Western Allies. The Italians found no reason to be grateful to anybody. But each side accepted the peace treaty because the worst had been avoided.

In the abstract, the F.T.T. compromise was an excellent solution. It recognized that no strictly "ethnic" line could be drawn fairly, or would make much sense if it could be. It took account of the need of the city for a flourishing port with an economic hinterland in Yugoslavia and central Europe. It guaranteed the civil and cultural rights of the people. It also created a special role for the United Nations, as the Security Council was to assure the integrity and independence of the F.T.T., and was to appoint its governor.[4]

Unfortunately, the carefully worked out "solution" took insufficient account of the division of Europe, and of the thickness of distrust that made it impossible for the USSR and the West even to agree on a governor for the F.T.T., which never came into being as a functioning political entity. This negative outcome on seemingly frivolous grounds was a symbol of the depth of the cold war even at that early stage, and another confirmation to Italy and Yugoslavia that the line between the two "temporary" zones of occupation and administration in the F.T.T.—Zone A (United States and United Kingdom) and Zone B (Yugoslavia)—was a segment of the line between two enormous aggregates of power on which they had no influence.

A "Danzig" on the Adriatic would probably have been no wondrous example of international administration, Italian-Yugoslav cooperation, or economic benefit for all. But if a functioning F.T.T. was not to come into being at all, the problem had to be considered more or less indefinitely unsolved, with no power able to change the *status quo* by force or hopeful of changing it by negotiation. It was in this atmosphere that the three Western Allies put forward their proposal of March 20,

---

[4] Treaty of Peace with Italy, signed February 10, 1947, U.S. Department of State Publication 2743 (Washington, D.C., Government Printing Office, 1947).

1948, that the whole area of the F.T.T. should go to Italy. The proposal was dictated by a desire to influence an election in Italy—admittedly a critical election, which it was feared the communists and their allies might win. It was, in fact, an empty gesture, because only force could have delivered Zone B to Italy. It naturally provoked further antagonism in Yugoslavia, but the Allies believed that Western relations with Yugoslavia were hopeless anyway. In that same year this belief proved to be wrong.

Yugoslavia's split with the Soviet Union changed the fundamentals of the Trieste problem, a fact which became apparent only gradually. The Western powers naturally welcomed the change in the international balance, which eased the military pressure on Italy and on their own position in the Mediterranean. They also benefited from the change in the position and outlook of Yugoslavia. Without the help of Moscow (meager as it had been in the past), Tito could not even hope to get Trieste. Yugoslavia was now on its own, and had to pay particular attention to the handling of its relations with the West, which were improving but were constantly troubled by the Trieste issue. The position of Italy, however, was also growing weaker, for its Western partners had less reason to back its claims once the threat of Soviet power in the Adriatic had receded, and they were making an investment in Yugoslavia's independence.

Despite these sea changes, the period 1948 to 1953 was one in which the problem remained essentially nonnegotiable. Zone A, which had by far the larger population because it included the city, remained under Anglo-American military government, and Yugoslav military government continued in Zone B. Italy kept reminding its allies of the promise of March 1948, and also pressed them for a larger Italian role in Zone A. Yugoslavia was, naturally, concerned about its hold on Zone B, and also insisted that there be no diminution of its rights and interests in Zone A. That was the basic reason for the violent outburst in Belgrade in Ocober 1953, when the Americans and British, under pressure from Rome and hoping to dispose of a burdensome and dangerous situation, proposed to withdraw their troops and hand over the occupation and administration of Zone A to Italy. A secret annex to their note to Rome said that the absence of a solution had become intolerable, that the intention of the two powers was to bring the two parties to a final settlement by creating this new *de facto* situation, and that they would not protest Yugoslavia's annexation of Zone B.[5] Tito replied publicly that his country would regard the entry of Italian troops into Zone A as aggression, and would respond with armed force. The two powers took him seriously and dropped their proposal, although they never formally withdrew it.

The underlying purpose of the Yugoslav reaction was to make the point beyond any question that no part of the disputed territory (the F.T.T.) could be disposed of, even provisionally, without consultation and agreement with Yugoslavia. The Yugoslavs' objection was more to the shock treatment than to the substance of the proposed solution, which Tito had told British Foreign Secretary Anthony Eden a year earlier he could accept, though he could not propose it. It was, in a way, a sign

[5] Text of public declaration in *Department of State Bulletin*, October 19, 1953, p. 529; on the annex, see Duroselle, *Le Conflit de Trieste*, p. 388.

INTRODUCTION

of improving relations with the West that Tito and his regime felt compelled to react so strongly against this reversion to the tactic of fait accompli in Italy's favor.

THE APPEARANCE OF FAVORING WINDS

The events of October 1953 cleared the air, and made all the parties rethink their positions. The fact that the British and Americans wanted to get out of Zone A in effect precipitated a new negotiation. By this time, too, the Trieste dispute was out of phase with the general international situation. Yugoslavia was under siege by the Soviet Union, which had not abandoned Stalin's campaign of pressure, even though Stalin himself was dead. Its relations with the Western powers were approaching the high point of cooperation, with military and economic aid now flowing regularly. The arms aid was being provided in the context of strategic plans whereby Yugoslav forces would guard the Ljubljana Gap, the gateway to Italy, in the event of a Soviet attack. Yugoslavia had concluded an entente (later to become an alliance) with Greece and Turkey, both members of NATO.

Nobody who was engaged in these developments wanted the Trieste dispute to spoil them. The Soviet Union, meanwhile, was engaged in bringing the dispute before the U.N. Security Council for precisely that purpose. But neither Rome nor Belgrade could take any initiative. Their public positions were irreconcilable, the burden of the past was too heavy. For each side there was a sense of security in holding to established and extreme positions so long as the other side's disposition to compromise, and even one's own, were unknown quantities.

THE STORY IN BRIEF

In these circumstances only a third party had any chance of testing whether the period of nonnegotiability might give way to one in which there was a reasonable chance for negotiation. It was apparent from the facts of the situation that no substantial change in the territorial *status quo* could be negotiated. The basic questions were whether the political climate in Italy would permit any Italian prime minister to renounce Zone B, even if he could simultaneously celebrate the return of Trieste to Italy, and whether the Yugoslav government could formally accept the loss of the city, or could be content with gaining nothing beyond what it already held. The third party would have to make a judgment on those points and then find a formula for bringing the disputants to a compromise agreement.

Who could that third party be? The Council of Foreign Ministers, which had drafted the peace treaty, was not suitable because the USSR was a member. Nobody wanted the Soviets brought back to an active role. Neither side was ready for some neutral mediator to assume the task; or, at any rate, there was no effort to find such an individual. Individually or as a group, the Western powers could not easily overcome the presumption of bias inherent in their closer association with Italy than with Yugoslavia, or their earlier support of Italy against Yugoslavia. The United States, Britain, and France, the three powers that had made the pro-Italian proposal of March 1948, had begun discussing what to do in the new circumstances of 1953, but the prospects of a five-nation conference or some similar device seemed most unpromising.

The solution that was found was a practical one, and it left France out. The United States and Britain were the occupying powers in Zone A. They could talk to

INTRODUCTION

Yugoslavia as the occupying power of Zone B, and they had bargaining power of their own in the decision to stay or to go and on what terms. They also had reasons of their own for wanting a solution: they wanted to reduce their own responsibilities, to see quiet in the area, to get Italy and Yugoslavia cooperating on defense, and to foreclose meddling by the Soviet Union. And they had the statesmanship to try a new tack, one which was quite the reverse of what they had done in October 1953.

THE COURSE OF THE NEGOTIATION

The brief account that follows is intended to give the main substance of the negotiations and the points on which their success hinged, as background for the interviews in which the negotiators themselves give their own views and judgments.

The story begins in early February 1954, with conversations between the American and British representatives (Llewellyn Thompson and Geoffrey Harrison) on one side and the Yugoslav representative (Vladimir Velebit) on the other. Their purpose was to reach agreement on terms that the Americans and British would then propose to Italy, urging their acceptance. Thompson's instructions from Washington were "to put the Trieste problem in the larger context of an over-all Italian-Yugoslav rapprochement which, ideally, would lead ultimately to Italian membership" in, or association with, the Turkish-Greek-Yugoslav defense pact then being negotiated. The Yugoslavs were to be impressed that the Americans and British were not thinking of a local settlement or of Italian-Yugoslav relations alone, "but rather of the political, military, and economic health of

THE STORY IN BRIEF

a key area which will have great significance for all of the free world and for the world-wide effort to throw back Soviet expansion." The costs of failure would be high, as would the benefits of success. The demonstration of cooperation between free countries in the area of Italy and Yugoslavia would be of profound significance in the eyes of the Kremlin, and, therefore, a package deal that would enable both sides to accept sacrifices in a Trieste settlement would put relations on a sound basis and serve the entire free world.

Within that general approach, Thompson was to press Yugoslavia to settle. To strengthen his persuasive powers he was authorized to remind the Yugoslavs that Tito himself had told Eden, in September 1952, that he could accept a territorial solution along the zonal boundary. He could also remind the Yugoslavs that if a negotiated solution were not forthcoming the United States and Britain would have no recourse but to go back to the October 8th declaration. The specific American proposals, however, were not for a border along the Zone A-Zone B line, but for one that would give Italy a coastal strip in Zone B, including all its major cities and ports, although Yugoslavia should have a suitable port area and secure access to it.[6]

As the talks began, the Yugoslavs, so far as they were exposed to this line of argument by Thompson, did not accept the idea that general interest in the security of the region required them to compromise on Trieste. On the contrary, Velebit took the line that Yugoslav rights were clear and unchallengeable. He started out with a

---

[6] Letter of instructions from Acting Secretary of State W. B. Smith to Ambassador Thompson, January 28, 1954 (National Archives, Washington, D.C., cited hereafter as NA, 750G. 00/1–2854). See Appendix C below.

INTRODUCTION

presentation of claims to virtually all of the F.T.T., including the city of Trieste. In time, when these claims were seen to be wholly unacceptable to the American and British negotiators, he came down to the only basis on which a deal could be made, essentially a Zone A-Zone B division with adjustments.

The tough bargaining was on the nature of the adjustments. Velebit remained quite firm in the early negotiations, causing Thompson and Harrison to contemplate such drastic steps as breaking off the talks, informing the Italians, appealing to Tito, or preparing to carry out the October 1953 proposal.[7] But none of these steps proved necessary. Velebit himself believed that in the end the only practicable agreement would be a split roughly along the boundary of the two zones, but he did not find it easy to get his government (which had Slovenes in many influential positions) to take the necessary steps in retreat. Along the way the Yugoslavs tried hard to get a substantial part of Zone A, and especially to push the line down to the sea for a port at Zaule (Žavlje) and Muggia (Milje) just southeast of Trieste, but they failed. The Americans and British tried to get Yugoslav consent to leave three coastal towns in Zone B—Koper (Capodistria), Izola (Isola), Piran (Pirano)—to Italy, but they failed. Once it was understood that the Yugoslavs had to forget about getting Zaule, it was obvious that any territorial gain they could make would be merely a face-saver.

In the end, agreement was reached on a line that gave Yugoslavia a small slice of Zone A and held open the possibility of offering Italy an even smaller piece of Zone B of no great use to anybody. Yugoslavia won

[7] Thompson telegrams to Department of State, London's 3488, February 13; and 3549, February 19, 1954 (NA 750G. 00/2-1354, and 2-1754).

THE STORY IN BRIEF

significant rights and concessions in the accompanying agreements on maintenance of the free port at Trieste, movement of people, minority rights, cultural centers, and concurrent settlement of Yugoslav financial claims on Italy.[8] The promise of economic aid from the United States and United Kingdom for port construction in Zone B, although not mentioned in the agreement, was a part of the package, and helped to seal Yugoslavia's agreement to it. Whether an offer or prospect of broader American aid to Yugoslavia, principally in much-needed wheat, also had a part in clinching the deal is a point on which differing conclusions have been expressed. Vladimir Velebit, who was in a good position to know, states in his interview that U.S. aid was not a factor in Yugoslavia's decision.[9]

On June 1, opening the second phase of the negotiations, Thompson and Harrison presented the draft terms to the chosen representative of Italy, Manlio Brosio, who had not even been kept informed of the course of the prior talks. He was given the text not as a take-it-or-leave-it proposition, but supposedly as a subject for genuine negotiation. Nevertheless, the Italians were given to understand that there was not much leeway for change, or the whole agreement would become unstuck. In general, Brosio was not displeased with the terms, but of course he was not going to refrain from trying to improve them. He was able to negotiate some modifications in the arrangements on nonterritorial mat-

[8] Text of "agreed record of positions reached" in London despatch no. 3920 to Department of State, June 2, 1954 (NA 750G. 00/6-254).

[9] Duroselle, *Le Conflit de Trieste* (pp. 412, 414) indicates that economic "pressure" was a factor in obtaining Yugoslavia's agreement to the territorial terms presented to Italy on June 1, 1954, *a point made by Anthony Eden, British Foreign Secretary at the time* (in *Full Circle*, Boston: Houghton Mifflin, 1960, pp. 207-208).

INTRODUCTION

ters (on which agreement was contingent on ultimate agreement to the whole package), but on the location of the border he ran up against a solid Anglo-American refusal to countenance any change.

Just as it was a matter of prestige for the Yugoslavs to get something a little better than a simple Zone A-Zone B split, so it became a matter of prestige for the Italians, who had in effect been offered Zone A in the previous October and felt they should have nothing less, to come out with a map that improved on the one handed to them. Not interested in the offer of useless territory in Zone B, they fixed on a small area in Zone A in the neighborhood of Punta Sottile (Tenki Rtič), part of the territory slated to go to Yugoslavia. It was on a piece of high ground overlooking the suburbs and port of Trieste, and therefore seemed in some way menacing. Neither Brosio nor his government would yield on this demand.

On this matter of a couple of square miles of rocky ground the whole negotiation came to a halt, with everything else ready for signature. Rome took it up at the highest diplomatic levels with Washington, making it an issue of confidence in Italian-American relations at a time when Secretary of State John Foster Dulles was especially anxious for Italian ratification of the European Defense Community treaty. Washington decided on a special mission to Tito, entrusting it to Robert Murphy. He was to go also to several other European capitals, but the main purpose was to seek an acceptable Trieste formula in Belgrade and in Rome.

Murphy was an experienced diplomat who knew Tito personally. He went to Yugoslavia bearing a friendly letter from President Eisenhower. The text of the letter is of considerable interest in the way in which it combines an appeal to Tito's wisdom and statesmanship that could bring the Trieste negotiations to a successful conclusion, reference to the larger issues of defense of "the free world of which our countries are part," and mention of current American aid programs to Yugoslavia and of "certain economic developments and emergencies" which Murphy was being asked to review with Tito "in a spirit of sympathy."[10]

The United States was then in the process of considering a Yugoslav request for food and had informed the Yugoslav government that Murphy would want to discuss outstanding problems, including wheat and economic aid as well as Trieste. Murphy was authorized to invoke, if necessary, the personal authority of the President in warning of a less sympathetic American attitude toward Yugoslav requests for economic and military aid in the future "if they refuse the concessions we seek" on Trieste.[11] But Murphy, though he discussed the wheat question with some Yugoslav officials, did not bring up the subject with Tito. The latter was well disposed anyway. He was not wrought up about the Trieste deadlock and did not really care about the Punta Sottile "rock pile." He wanted a settlement, so he gave the Italians a choice: they could have most of the Punta Sottile area, leaving a small settlement just south of it, Lazzaretto (Lazaret), to Yugoslavia and getting a small piece of territory in Zone B; or they could take both Punta Sottile and Lazzaretto and give up any compensation in Zone B. Murphy took this proposition to Rome. Italy

---

[10] Text of the letter is in Appendix B below. The initiative for the letter came from the State Department. The permission of the President (then in Denver) and the concurrence of Secretary Dulles (then in the Far East) were then sought and obtained.

[11] Telegrams from Acting Secretary Smith to Eisenhower and to Dulles, September 3, 1954 (NA 750G. 00/9–354).

INTRODUCTION

chose the second alternative, and the Trieste dispute was settled.

It was, rather, "provisionally" settled. The Italian government did not want a settlement with the label of "permanent" on it because of a natural desire to tell its people that nothing had been finally and irrevocably given away. Yugoslavia wanted the deal to be final, to forestall future Italian claims and agitation. In fact, it could not be made final without a revision of the Italian peace treaty, to which many states, including the USSR, were parties. So what happened, in the document the four parties signed on October 5, 1954,[12] was the termination of military government in the territories of the F.T.T. and the assumption of governing authority by civil administrations of Italy and Yugoslavia on their respective sides of the agreed new line. The question of sovereignty and finality was avoided. But the Western powers stated publicly that they would give no support to claims of either Yugoslavia or Italy to territory under the sovereignty or administration of the other. Both parties wanted the deal to stick, and they held to it after it was made. What had been an unsolvable, nonnegotiable territorial dispute disappeared from the world's agenda of conflict, although the potential for its revival was not totally extinguished.[13]

[12] Memorandum of Understanding between the governments of Italy, the United Kingdom of Great Britain and Northern Ireland, the United States of America and Yugoslavia regarding the Free Territory of Trieste (United Nations, *Treaty Series*, vol. 235, 1956, no. 3297). See Appendix A below.

[13] In the exchanges of notes accompanying the flare-up of the dispute in the spring of 1974, Italy referred to "the Italian territory designated as Zone B of the F.T.T.," and Yugoslavia replied that this was in fact sovereign Yugoslav territory by virtue of the peace treaty and the agreement of 1954. Both positions were legally unsound. See *Yugoslav Survey* (Belgrade), 15, no. 2 (May 1954), 131–142.

THE STORY IN BRIEF

The parties to the agreement notified the President of the United Nations Security Council, who in turn notified its members. The Soviet Union, in contrast to its threats of one year before, chose to raise no objectins. Andrei Vyshinsky, indeed, officially informed the council that his government accepted the agreement because it would restore normal relations between Italy and Yugoslavia and contribute to a lessening of tensions in that part of Europe.[14] There was scarcely a ripple on the international waters. The Italian peace treaty was not amended. And the provisional has endured.

[14] U.N. Security Council, Official Records, S/3305, October 13, 1954.

CHAPTER ONE

The American Negotiator, Llewellyn E. Thompson

In November 1971 Llewellyn Thompson was interviewed in his home in Washington, D.C., by Joseph E. Johnson and John C. Campbell, both of whom were old personal friends. Although seriously ill at the time, Thompson cooperated fully in the enterprise because he shared the belief that the Trieste negotiation merited detailed study, of which an indispensable ingredient was the first-hand evidence of the participants.

On some points he frankly conceded that his memory did not serve him well, and he did not wish to go beyond his area of certain knowledge. In general, his remarks were more guarded than those of the other participants. This was not the result of his illness, but reflected his usual restraint in discussing official matters and his desire to avoid doing injury to others. Thompson remained in active service virtually to the end of his life. He did not write his memoirs, and did not intend to, believing they would inevitably involve secrets that were not his to give out.

The diplomatic career that Thompson began in 1929 was long and distinguished. He held diplomatic posts in Colombo, Geneva, and Moscow, and the Soviet desk in the Department of State, before acting as an adviser to the Secretary of State at a wide range of international meetings, including the San Francisco Conference in 1945, the Berlin Conference in 1945 and the Council of

Foreign Ministers in London in 1945. He participated in the negotiations on the Italian peace treaty, where Trieste was interminably discussed and ultimately settled by a compromise—the Free Territory—which did not work. It was during his later service as Ambassador to Austria, a post he held from 1952 to 1955, that he participated in the final and successful phase of the Trieste negotiations.

During his two periods of service as Ambassador to the Soviet Union, 1957 to 1962 and 1967 to 1969, Thompson's remarkable diplomatic intelligence and skills became well known. But well before then he had won the admiration of his professional colleagues. Of the various architects of the Trieste settlement he probably contributed the most. As representative of the government having the greatest weight with the two contending parties, but no power to impose a solution, he used his influence with wisdom and restraint. Throughout the proceedings he had the confidence of his fellow negotiators.

On the American side of the enterprise his was by far the leading role. Secretary Dulles followed the negotiations but not in detail, approving the broad strategy, and backing his principal negotiator on his chosen tactics. Clare Boothe Luce and James Riddleberger, Ambassadors in Rome and Belgrade respectively, did well in their supporting roles; Mrs. Luce was instrumental in getting the process started, and also in the initiative for the Murphy mission. Murphy himself, with his customary aplomb, brought off the final success. But the greatest credit must go to Thompson.

Less than three months after this interview was completed, on February 6, 1972, Llewellyn Thompson died of cancer.

LLEWELLYN E. THOMPSON

QUESTION: If you cast your mind back to the time when your part in the negotiations started, which I take it would be around December 1953, can you talk a bit about the situation at that time between the two parties, and the attitudes of the British, ourselves, and of course the French, who were in the picture, to indicate what was the situation from which the decision came to start the special mediatory negotiation which began in January 1954? Was there a feeling of urgency at that time that a negotiation of this new type had to begin?

THOMPSON: Well, I was then stationed in Vienna, and had very little to do with the negotiations. I understand Mrs. Luce kept pounding away to try to get them started. That was really almost her only role, but it was an important one. As you recall, there had been a number of attempts at different levels, including high ones, to settle this problem. They had all failed, I think, because the negotiations were more or less public, or leaked to the public, so that each side had pressure on it to take a firm position from which it could not retreat. I think the real basis for the success of the negotiations I was involved in was their secrecy. I went to London and hid out really successfully for three months, though it gradually became known by some people that I was there.

QUESTION: When did you first go to London?

THOMPSON: Early in January 1954, just before the negotiations started.

QUESTION: Do you have any recollection of the reasons why you and Harrison were the ones chosen for this? In your case was it because of your prior experience with the Yugoslavs or other negotiations or because you could be more easily disguised?

THOMPSON: I think actually it was not very easy to disguise me. I believe it was that they were looking for somebody they thought could handle it. So many other people were tied up or unsuitable for one reason or another. They picked me because of the experience I had, and, of course too, there was the Russian reaction to this. That was somewhat involved, I guess. It was hard to get away from Vienna, however, because meetings on the state treaty were still going on.

QUESTION: Did you have a set of instructions from the State Department?

THOMPSON: Yes, they were hopeless. That became quite clear to me.

QUESTION: Hopeless?

THOMPSON: Basically they were favorable to Italy and did not give us room to negotiate with the Yugoslavs. Also, the department sent over to London a huge delegation, including Phil Mosely [Philip E. Mosely, United States Representative to the 1946 Commission for Investigation of the Yugoslav-Italian Boundary], who was to serve as a territorial expert, a military representative, and others. So when we started, both sides—the British and the Americans on one side and the Yugoslavs on the other—had quite high-powered delegations. The Yugoslavs opened with long statements of their claims, and quite clearly they were speaking for the record. These were polemical speeches. We were getting absolutely nowhere, so one day I suggested to Harrison that we talk to Velebit alone. He readily agreed, and so did Velebit. We went to Velebit's house, and just the three of us sat down with nobody else present.

QUESTION: This was after a couple of weeks?

THOMPSON: Yes. At that time we still kept our delegations in London, but this new tack was so successful—we did more in this one session than we had done in the previous two weeks—that we just continued on that basis thereafter. I don't know the exact period of time, but within a relatively short time we just dismissed our delegations and carried on—the three of us.

QUESTION: Was that when Velebit began to show some indication of what the Yugoslavs really would take, rather than what they were demanding?

THOMPSON: Yes, except that Velebit was always very discreet. I'll give you one example of the problem. It eventually boiled down to a situation in which, if he had told us what was bothering him in the negotiation far earlier, we might have moved forward more rapidly. The problem was that our proposals, which I had from Washington, gave the whole coastline, in Zone B as well as Zone A, to Italy, but all the hinterland said Yugoslavia on the map. The part you would color red for Yugoslavia was big compared to the part you would color green for Italy, but each time I would summarize the pros and cons, Velebit would dismiss the concession as not worth very much. I suddenly realized that practically all the coastal people were fishermen. If we had settled the thing the way we had it drawn, for the Yugoslavs to continue their profession of fishing, they would have had to opt for Italy and move over, and this would have been very embarrassing to the Yugoslavs—to have an exodus of Yugoslavs into Italy. So I tried this out on the department: a new deal in which I reshuffled the proposals. The department resisted this change at first but finally let it go forward, and the minute it did, Velebit said, "I will recommend to my government that they accept this."

QUESTION: You gave up the idea of holding those towns in Zone B, Piran, Koper, and Izola, for Italy?

THOMPSON: As I recall it, we had wanted to save for Italy those towns in Zone B because they were Italian in population. And the Yugoslavs, I gather, really could not take that. They wanted to have that coast. I think also that when it became clear they were going to have to give up Trieste itself, there was the question of an alternative port that could be developed. They did not get the one they wanted, but they did keep the Zone B ports, and in the final deal they got a bit of Zone A. But I frankly don't remember the details now.

When we finally got Yugoslav agreement on a territorial bargain, the Yugoslavs proposed that we put forward a position which was worse for Italy than the one we had agreed upon, so that we could have a concession to make to the Italians. But we were afraid to do that for fear it would leak, and so we refused. Then when we went to the Italians, Brosio and the Italian government felt that to save face they had to get some further concession. Otherwise they said they would be accepting a *diktat*. Actually I think they were quite pleased with what we had gotten for them. It was much more than they had expected. But they still felt, as the Yugoslavs and all of us had anticipated, that they had to get something more. That's when Murphy went to Yugoslavia to get for Italy what turned out to be a place just a few city blocks in size overlooking Trieste. Their argument was that a man could sit up there with a rifle and shoot at Trieste. It was nonsense. I mean, it was just purely a face-saving thing. Getting it was the final thing that clinched the whole negotiation.

QUESTION: Was the Murphy mission a kind of playing out of a final action which everybody knew would succeed, or was the thing really hanging between success or failure?

THOMPSON: The Yugoslavs felt, Velebit made quite clear, that they had made their absolutely maximum concessions, and more too, and that they were not going to give anything more. So it was a real question of whether they would listen to this final proposal at all.

QUESTION: The Italians were sitting on the sidelines during the Yugoslav part of the negotiations. Were they kept entirely in the dark? Had anybody let anything out to them or did they just wait?

THOMPSON: Neither Harrison nor I did, and I think officially neither of our governments did. Now, whether Mrs. Luce was slipping them something or not, I don't know. I don't think so, because we made quite a point of keeping things secret, and from Brosio's reaction when we presented him with the proposals, we had the impression he had not known what was going on. There was one period in the middle of the negotiations when somebody, I think it was an Italian, sounded off and the Yugoslavs replied, and this set the negotiations back by a couple of months. It took us a couple of months to get over this surfacing of issues.

QUESTION: Was this before you went into the three-man negotiation?

THOMPSON: No. This was the period when we were in it, but anyway, the Yugoslavs then dug in, and it was very hard to get them to move again. It showed how difficult it became with publicity, how essential it was that the negotiations be secret. So that I don't think the Italians really knew anything of our talks with Velebit. They must have done a lot of guesswork, and they probably picked up a little bit, but they had no real knowledge, as far as I know, as to what was going on.

QUESTION: You spoke of Brosio's reaction to the terms you got. Did you get the idea from him that basically there could be a deal on those terms?

THOMPSON: Sure.

QUESTION: But they just wanted something to save face—a little more so that they could say they negotiated?

THOMPSON: He pretended, of course, that this was a terrible settlement, but you could tell the way he reacted, without saying so, that they were quite pleased with what we had worked out.

QUESTION: What you had worked out initially was Zone A for the Italians, Zone B for the Yugoslavs, with a little slice of Zone A also going to the Yugoslavs. Would you agree that, although there were some discussions of parts of Zone B going to them, when it came down to it the Italians did not really care much whether they got a few useless square feet in Zone B as long as they got Trieste and the southern suburbs?

THOMPSON: As I say, I am very vague on this now. I would not want to commit myself to what the terms were.

QUESTION: Of course, the essential bargain was the status quo except for a very slight change enabling the Yugoslavs to get something they had not been able to get before for their people. Right?

THOMPSON: Not the status quo. The Italians really did not have Trieste. We had it. We, the Italians, and Yugoslavs were all cultivating the Triestini by special concessions of all kinds. They got more bread and lower electricity prices from the Italians than anybody else. We were putting in all kinds of aid projects. In fact we were hard pressed to find things to spend money on. And of course the minute the Italians got Trieste, they transferred a lot of their shipbuilding contracts to Genoa or other places, and the people of Trieste, I think, regretted the deal very shortly. There were some things that helped a lot. One of them was enabling the people to go back and forth with a minimum of formality, and this worked out very well.

QUESTION: One of the things that interests me is how often in negotiations there is an added factor such as the introduction of a new person—in this case Bob Murphy's going to Belgrade to talk about a specific thing rather than having it done by you. I suppose that was because it was felt Tito had to be talked to directly about the settlement?

THOMPSON: That's right.

QUESTION: I know that, when I [Joseph E. Johnson] was involved in one of the negotiations on the Middle East, a special trip was made by somebody from the White House to see how things were going before the United States made up its mind as to how far it was going to push in a particular line. So side trips can be extremely important. They sometimes do not even appear in the record of the negotiation. Does Murphy's trip appear in the record?

THOMPSON: No, but this trip was well known.

QUESTION: It was well known? Was the public story that Bob was going to Belgrade for some other reason than this?

THOMPSON: I think so, yes.

QUESTION: Is it your understanding that the Murphy trip was really a part of the same negotiation, in the sense that there was just one point which could not be put over and this was the way chosen to do it?

THOMPSON: Yes, to extract one small concession out of the Yugoslavs.

QUESTION: There is another question, and that is to what extent in talking to both sides you brought in anything such as aid to Yugoslavia or something for Italy to help the negotiations along? Maybe this is what you were referring to as what we—the British and ourselves—might be able to do to make them more receptive to the Trieste agreement.

THOMPSON: Well, there were some things of that nature. One of the things, as I recall, was that there were certain trade arrangements that were worked out that were favorable to the Yugoslavs, and which meant that if they broke the agreement or did not carry it out, they would lose the advantage that was involved. This was really a sideline affair.

QUESTION: Arrangements between Trieste and Yugoslavia?

THOMPSON: Between Italy and Yugoslavia. It gave the Yugoslavs a reason to fulfill the agreement and stick by it.

QUESTION: Another issue which you also touched upon had to do with whether these negotiations could be carried all the way through without being damaged by something happening on the scene, so to speak, in the politics of either one of the two countries, something in their relations with each other or public statements which put the other side in a difficult position. Do you recall any instances when there was the possibility of a breakdown in the negotiations?

THOMPSON: There was only one time when negotiations broke off, to my knowledge. That was quite damaging. You recall that there was a long history of negotiations. Everybody and his brother had tried it, and had not succeeded. I think we hit it at a terribly favorable time as far as both sides were concerned, in that they both wanted to get this thing settled.

QUESTION: Well, they must have, to have been willing

to keep quiet. Isn't it true that if you don't want an agreement, you can always leak?

THOMPSON: Exactly. I was going to say that you must remember we negotiated almost exclusively with the Yugoslavs. Out of the eight months, I think we spent the first five with the Yugoslavs. It was only then that we presented the proposals to the Italians. Of course we had to go back to the Yugoslavs toward the end.

QUESTION: You said that during the first three or four months you were in London people did not even know you were there.

THOMPSON: That's right. I told everybody I was buying clothes, and I was. But it was an excuse.

QUESTION: Brosio knew you were in London?

THOMPSON: Yes.

QUESTION: Why was it decided to do the negotiating in London?

THOMPSON: Well, there was a four-power conference going on in Berlin. For the talks on Trieste we and the British wanted a place that was neutral so far as Italy and Yugoslavia were concerned. Harrison had a pretty heavy job in the Foreign Office which they did not want to release him from, so he was able to carry on his regular job and negotiate on the side more or less. This is one reason why, though it may sound a little immodest, a lot of the work fell to me because I had full time and he did not. But he was very good and we had no difficulties at all.

QUESTION: You reported, I gather, from time to time to your own governments. Did you both have a pretty free hand?

THOMPSON: Well, at the start I was bound by these absurd instructions, and I had to play that hand out for a long time. I had to keep going back, trying to get my instructions changed to work out something that was realistic, particularly the territorial deal which at the end was the real basis for the agreement.

QUESTION: Were these instructions absurd in the sense that they were asking the Yugoslavs to give up so much that it just did not make real negotiation possible?

THOMPSON: More or less, yes. It just did not fit.

QUESTION: With the Yugoslavs or the Italians?

THOMPSON: The Yugoslavs. Our original position was so pro-Italian there was just no chance of Yugoslavia buying it.

QUESTION: It started out with you, in effect, trying to sell the Italian position to the Yugoslavs. But as you say, Yugoslavia could not be expected to give up a large part of Zone B, as well as Trieste itself and all of Zone A.

You remember the October 1953 pronouncement that we were to hand over Zone A to the Italians, and how the Yugoslavs exploded in protest against that as settling without even consulting them. But basically they were not so opposed to a rough Zone A-Zone B deal, for that is what they accepted in the end. Would you agree that they just would not accept it as something dictated to them, that they wanted to negotiate?

THOMPSON: I think it was clear to them in 1954 that we were not going to change our basic position once we had jiggled the territorial thing around.

QUESTION: When you talked to me the other day you used the word *diktat* and at that time I thought that you were referring to the Yugoslav reaction at one point or another. But you used the word a few minutes ago in describing how the Italians would not take the solution you worked out with Velebit because it looked like a dictated one. In both cases, in other words, was there the appearance of a *diktat* at different times?

THOMPSON: I do not know much about the question of the Yugoslavs, so far as our talks in 1954 were concerned, but the Italians felt that if they could not get any change made in the terms, they were accepting a dictated settlement.

QUESTION: Suppose we consider the Yugoslav side of it outside the negotiations as it bears on their position and policy. In October 1953, when Dulles and the British tried to settle the dispute, more or less by their own decision, the Yugoslavs not only indignantly rejected the proposal but also rioted and tore up the U.S.I.S. [United States Information Service] building in Belgrade, and so forth. These events created something of a crisis in relations between Yugoslavia and the two occupying Western powers. Do you think that Tito at that time felt that the strong Yugoslav reaction, while perhaps salutary from their point of view, had gone too far and might really queer his relations with us at a time when he needed our aid very much? In that event in January 1954 they might have been in a much more receptive mood, I should think, for real negotiations than they were at the time of the crisis of the previous October.

THOMPSON: Maybe. They did not give any glimmer of it in the first months of the negotiations. They took a very rigid position.

QUESTION: Did they, in fact, ask for large chunks of Zone A?

THOMPSON: Well, they wanted Trieste itself. They had prepared a case in great detail.

QUESTION: Did you get an impression from Velebit that they were concerned about their relations with us because of their relations with the Soviets?

THOMPSON: I do not think so, other than just the whole general tenor of the negotiations.

QUESTION: That year, 1954, was the time when they began to slide away from their very close relations with us, which had gone even to the point of talking about military plans. It was late 1954 when you began to hear the conciliatory noises both on their side and the Soviet side which led up to the visit of Nikita Khrushchev, who had just achieved the top spot in the Soviet Union and had decided on a new line to Yugoslavia, to Belgrade in 1955. How do you think Yugoslav attitudes toward the Soviets and ourselves may have affected their willingness to make a deal on Trieste at that time?

THOMPSON: I just don't know. Undoubtedly there were a lot of things cranked into the decisions that they made.

QUESTION: Did they give Velebit a good deal of flexibility in negotiating? Do you have any impression of that?

THOMPSON: Well, I don't think he was allowed to make any concessions ad hoc. He had to go back and get instructions for it, as we did. But he could at least listen to suggestions and did not automatically turn them down.

QUESTION: From what you say about their stiffness in the early part of the negotiations it sounds as if they were not particularly influenced, at least in early 1954, by other considerations in their relations with us and the Soviet Union. Is that correct?

THOMPSON: That's right. They just did not feel they could bend at all at that stage.

QUESTION: Turning to the American side of the negotiation, who had a hand in it besides yourself?

THOMPSON: They restricted my cables quite closely, so there were not too many people who knew about the talks and could leak information the way it often happens.

QUESTION: Were your cables sent to our embassy in Belgrade?

THOMPSON: Yes. I think most of them.

QUESTION: Who was in Belgrade at that time?

THOMPSON: Jimmy Riddleberger [James Riddleberger, United States Ambassador to Yugoslavia, 1953–1958].

QUESTION: Did he come to London at any time?

THOMPSON: No. Jimmy played practically no role. He had almost no comments. Nor did Clare Luce.

QUESTION: Do you agree that much credit was given to her at the end?

THOMPSON: Yes.

QUESTION: I want to ask you about the relative importance of the questions that were under discussion. Did you feel that the tougher question was the territorial one, or was it whether there should be a permanent or provisional arrangement?

THOMPSON: Oh, I think it was the territorial question that was the hardest for them, because the way they looked at it they had to defend their own people. And they knew the way the press would play it, and so on.

QUESTION: On both sides? Or are you talking mainly about the Yugoslavs?

THOMPSON: Mainly about the Yugoslavs, but on both sides. To the Italians, as long as they got Trieste—and got it without any caveats or restrictions—that was really the important thing for them.

QUESTION: No condominium or anything of the kind?

THOMPSON: No.

QUESTION: The Italian government changed three times or more during this period. Did that make any difference? I gather Scelba [Mario Scelba, Italian Prime Minister, 1954–1955] was a bit more willing, maybe because he was more confident of his position, to consider concessions than the others.

THOMPSON: Well, again, none of these governments except the last one, Scelba's, had anything to do with the London negotiations, because they were not involved. We were not talking to them. So it did not make any difference.

QUESTION: Isn't it rather unusual for a government to leave in the hands of other governments so much of the negotiations involving territory it cared about?

THOMPSON: I suppose the fact that we were on the spot and were occupying and administering Zone A made us somewhat partisan, which in a sense we were. Also, I think the Italians themselves knew that if too many people knew about the negotiations in progress, there would be positions taken which would be harmful. Therefore they never pressed us—at least Brosio never did—except in general terms. They never pressed us for any details.

QUESTION: Did they have much choice? Of course they always had the alternative of not agreeing and hoping for something better later on, since they were, after all, an ally of the two occupying powers, and the Yugoslavs were not. But I gather from the account which J. B. Duroselle wrote in his book, the Italians seemed to feel that time might be working the other way—for the Yugoslavs—and if they did not get an agreement then they might not even get Trieste. In that case they had some real reason to come to terms.

THOMPSON: The Yugoslavs were building up their military strength, and the Russians were a factor, I suppose, in the Italians' thinking; possibly they thought that at some stage the Russians might get together with the Yugoslavs.

QUESTION: Suppose we consider now the method of negotiation you used, which I guess is unique. I cannot find any good parallel to it anywhere. Do you feel that the way you did it was somehow the key to success? Was this a means of solving the problem while, let us say, a conference of four or five or some other method would have failed? Was this method so suited to the occasion?

THOMPSON: Negotiating with both parties at the same time would have failed if it had gone long enough. They would each have had to take positions that would have been hard to retreat from, because after all this whole thing was very much an internal political question in Italy. There was the powerful Christian Democratic party, with strong views about what should be done, and so on. So I think for that reason Brosio realized it was better for them not to be involved at the first stage. It would have stirred up internal politics in Italy.

QUESTION: What if it had been done the other way around, talking to the Italians first?

THOMPSON: No, I do not think that would have worked.

QUESTION: Did the procedure chosen seem to be called for by the situation that then existed?

THOMPSON: I think that's right. We realized that the Italians were our allies and could be asked to be patient; and that the Yugoslavs would not have taken that role. If we had started with Italy, I'm sure the thing would have blown open.

QUESTION: Well, it succeeded the way you did it. I recall that Mr. Dulles at the time was so pleased with the success that he thought the formula could be used elsewhere, with the Arabs and Israel, for example. Do you regard the method as a general tool or instrument of diplomacy that could be applied in other cases, or was it so specific that the lessons are for this particular question and not broader?

THOMPSON: I think the main lesson is the necessity of negotiating in secret on things of this sort, particularly anything that involves territory, because the moment a government takes a public position on a territorial issue, a retreat is almost impossible. On the other hand, it is hard to envisage a situation—except possibly the Arab-Israeli one—in which two outside powers could get together and work out a settlement through separate negotiations with the parties. In a sense, we were trying to do it ourselves unilaterally with the Rogers proposal for "proximity talks" between Arab and Israeli representatives. But I think big conferences with big delegations are hopeless when it comes to issues of this kind, where national prestige is involved, and so on. Nations are bound to make high-sounding polemical speeches which make negotiations very difficult indeed.

QUESTION: The two outside powers had a special, almost unique, relationship to this negotiation, in the fact that they had their own troops stationed in a good part of the territory in dispute. The Americans and the British, because of the presence of their troops, were involved as they have not been involved in the Middle East situation, for example. Do you think that made much of a difference?

THOMPSON: Yes, obviously.

QUESTION: Another consideration is that in this kind of operation it is obvious there has to be considerable confidence between the people in the middle, whether one power or two, and the parties to the dispute. We were in a position to talk to both the Italians and Yugoslavs in different ways, but in ways that gave us some authority with each. The difficulty with the Arabs and Israel is that situation has not existed in the same degree. Do you agree?

THOMPSON: That is right.

QUESTION: What became history after this deal was made, perhaps unexpectedly, was not only the success of the negotiation, but also what it led to—namely, that the settlement of a quarrel that had been going on since World War I brought Italy and Yugoslavia into a period of really good relations. The agreement worked out in a way which exceeded everybody's hopes, and in that sense has added luster. I wonder whether at the time the idea of what the agreement could produce went as far as what took place later on?

THOMPSON: I guess not quite, except that we tried to build into the agreement elements which would make it in the interest of both parties to continue.

QUESTION: Those elements are not all recorded in the formal agreement, are they? Some were side agreements, as you suggested, in trade and other things. Were all those written by you in London too?

THOMPSON: I do not know about "written," but they were worked out.

QUESTION: Any full study of what the significance of the agreement was should take account of everything that bears on the future relationship of the countries. Some results are still appearing. Tito visited Italy for the first time in the spring of 1971. He even saw the pope. The reaction in both countries, I thought, was fascinating in the light of history. Another related case or issue, in a sense, is the old Alto Adige question [the Italian-Austrian controversy over the province of Alto Adige, or south Tyrol], which has not been solved by any means with such success and is still pretty much before the two countries, Italy and Austria. But the Trieste agreement proved to be an example to follow.

THOMPSON: I think they have it pretty well on the way to solution. I get that impression both from the Austrians and the Italians.

QUESTION: It was very tense about the same time that you were dealing with Trieste.

THOMPSON: They had reached an agreement but the agreement kept unraveling.

QUESTION: Another thing that strikes me about the timing of the Trieste agreement is, again, the role of the Soviet Union. The deal was made, it seems to me, at about the last possible moment before the Yugoslavs again began criticizing both camps in a way in which, with the heavy emphasis on nonalignment, might have ruled it out. In any case they might have been more reluctant to make a deal with Italy in 1955 than they were in 1954 when they were still putting a great deal of emphasis on the need for good relations with the West. What do you think?

THOMPSON: That was the year before Bandung [a conference of Asian and African countries organized by President Sukarno of Indonesia], wasn't it?

QUESTION: Bandung was in 1955 and by then a lot of things had happened. 1954 was perhaps a year when this could be done, and it could not be done either earlier or later.

THOMPSON: You know how our own government works: the number of things that go into making a decision, internal situations and what not. I think we were lucky in our timing. Bureaucracy hampered us, but not decisively.

LLEWELLYN E. THOMPSON

QUESTION: I was interested to learn how highly Secretary Dulles valued the diplomatic success which your negotiations achieved and of his hope that he might use this technique on the Middle East conflict.

THOMPSON: Actually, when it came to the following election campaign, the three foreign policy successes that the Republican party emphasized were the Trieste agreement, the Austrian state treaty, and relations with the Soviet Union, all of which I had something to do with, although I had no partisan role.

QUESTION: There is one more related point here, and that is Secretary Dulles' own part in this negotiation. Was it significant? Did he have a role in encouraging you to get started on it? Did he stay out of it until it was finished and then congratulate everybody, or did he have something to say when it was going on?

THOMPSON: Well, at the very start of it he was tied up with the Berlin talks and had little to do with it. At the end, I suspect he had undoubtedly quite a lot to do with it. Everyone referred to him. But I have no way of knowing that. I had a very, very nice cable from him when the dispute was over.

QUESTION: Do you have any remarks, not in answer to questions, that occur to you about this negotiation or negotiations in general?

THOMPSON: I don't think I have any on negotiations themselves. One point I should like to emphasize is that there were absolutely no behind-the-scenes attempts by the British or us to undercut the other, for example by going to the Yugoslavs and saying, "I think you can get the Americans (or the British) to do this or that." As far as I know there was none of that, or just a slight amount at one stage, and we did none at all. Harrison was a very loyal colleague in working together with me.

On negotiations in general I give a lecture occasionally to the Foreign Service Institute, particularly on negotiating with the Russians, but it is all off the record. There are some techniques involved in negotiations that I suppose have some general applicability, particularly with the Soviets. For example, it is important to avoid surprises. Something like the "Open Skies" proposal [President Eisenhower's proposal that reconnaissance flights be freely permitted on both sides] was a great mistake to have sprung on them in 1955 at Geneva. I think if we had prepared the way for it we might have gotten it across, but springing it that way ruined the chances. It is always good to let the Russians know in advance so they can get an issue up to the Politburo and get a decision that they can approve, because without it their negotiators are helpless. Also, you cannot change positions with them too much, because their people cannot go to the Politburo every day the way we can go to the White House if we need to. It is not always easy for us to do it, but it is a lot harder for them to keep bringing up a new position, new details, and so on.

QUESTION: Did this one negotiation with the Yugoslavs give you enough parallels to negotiating with the Russians to be able to make any comparisons?

THOMPSON: No, not really. There was only the one element of secrecy: public agreements secretly arrived at.

CHAPTER TWO

The British Negotiator, Geoffrey W. Harrison

Sir Geoffrey Harrison discussed his participation in the Trieste negotiations in London with John C. Campbell in April of 1972. A person whom many would call the "consummate diplomat"—and indeed both Manlio Brosio and Vladimir Velebit noted how their respect for his competence, as well as for Llewellyn Thompson's, grew during the course of the negotiations—Harrison assumed the task of representing his government while serving as Assistant Undersecretary at the Foreign Office. He kept his Foreign Secretary, Anthony Eden, currently informed of the course of the talks, and Eden occasionally chipped in by having a conversation with Velebit or Brosio. But the day-to-day responsibility rested with Harrison, and he exercised it with competence and finesse.

Harrison describes the background for beginning the Trieste negotiation which "admittedly at that stage was regarded as rather a forlorn hope." His analysis, more rounded than Thompson's, places the talks and eventual settlement in the context of the politics of the day and traces the evolution of the discussions from the tense days of October 1953 to the final settlement one year later. He stresses the element of timing, the fact that by 1954 both sides were ready to accept a compromise as preferable to the continuance of a sterile and dangerous dispute. Thus he is modest in his evaluation of what diplomacy alone could and did accomplish.

One key to the success of the middleman role played by Britain and the United States was the harmony achieved by Harrison and Thompson. The policies of the two governments were roughly the same on the question of Trieste, but there were some differences in their relationships both with Italy and with Yugoslavia, and the personal relations between Eden and Dulles were anything but harmonious. It is greatly to Harrison's and Thompson's credit that they achieved such good teamwork that they could not be played off against one another. It was more than just the operation of the "old boy" network of British and American diplomats stemming from wartime and postwar collaboration.

The strategies and interpretations Harrison offers here stem from his keen recollection of the Trieste negotiations and his long experience in diplomatic matters. He entered the Foreign Service in 1932 and held posts in Tokyo, Berlin, Brussels, and Moscow before serving in the post he held during the Trieste talks. Later in his career, he served as Ambassador to Iran, Brazil, and the Soviet Union before retiring from diplomatic service in 1968.

Sir Geoffrey Harrison currently resides near Horsham in Sussex, England.

QUESTION: Sir Geoffrey, before we get into some of our questions, perhaps we might begin by recalling where the question of Trieste stood at the end of 1953 when you came into the picture. There had been, of course, the attempt in March 1948 on the part of the Western powers to declare that the whole Free Territory should go to Italy, which was not turned into fact. More recently, on October 8, 1953, there had been a declaration of the British and Americans that they were prepared to turn over Zone A to Italian administration, an act which the Yugoslavs violently protested by rioting in Belgrade against the Americans and British, and which therefore did not go forward.

The result was that at the close of 1953 there was discussion among the British, the Americans, and the French as to what steps they would take next to attempt to achieve a settlement. It was at this moment that suggestions were made that the British and Americans, presumably because they were the two powers who had troops in Zone A, might play a special role with the Italians and Yugoslavs, attempting to mediate between them. At this time, you were named to represent the U.K. for this purpose. Do you recall when and how you were given this assignment—why you were chosen, why London was chosen as the point for negotiation, and what your original instructions were in going into this assignment?

HARRISON: Well, I was chosen as the British representative because I was the Assistant Undersecretary in charge of affairs in that part of the world, among others, and I was regarded as the appropriate person to take on what admittedly at that stage was regarded as rather a forlorn hope. London and Washington were the possible venues, if I remember rightly, for the talks, and I think London was selected because it was thought that since secrecy was an important element, it might be easier to keep secrets and to keep the meeting secret in London rather than in Washington.

QUESTION: What instructions did you have other than just to listen to both sides? Did they involve more than going to talk to the Yugoslavs first?

BRITISH NEGOTIATOR

HARRISON: Yes. I think that the instructions were a little bit more precise than that, because, if I remember rightly, a procedure had been proposed, probably toward the end of 1953—I think by Washington—for a three or four stage program to do three things. The first step was to try to get Italian-Yugoslav relations normalized after the extremely tense situation with troop movements which had arisen after the October 8 proposal. The second part of the program was to eliminate, if possible, Soviet intervention in the Trieste situation: the Soviet Union was being very active in the United Nations and it was felt that this was not going to be a helpful intervention from the point of view of achieving any kind of settlement. The third leg of the program was to get talks started between Italy and Yugoslavia. That part of the program was the one in which I was involved, trying to work out the technique by which we could, if possible, bring the Italians and the Yugoslavs to a settlement.

In this we foresaw three stages—and by "we" I mean the American and British governments—because when the suggestions for handling the situation were put to the French, to Mr. Bidault [Georges Bidault, French Minister of Foreign Affairs, 1953–1954], if I remember rightly, the French were happy to contract out. So what happened was that Washington and London agreed on a program which would consist of the following: we would start by having tripartite talks between the Americans, the British, and the Yugoslavs, being the Allied military government and Yugoslav government in Zones A and B, respectively. We would work as far as we could with the Yugoslavs toward reaching some proposals which they could accept, and which we, the British and Americans, thought that we could reasonably put to the

Italians, and, if we were making reasonable progress we would, as the third stage of the program, act as intermediaries between the Italians and the Yugoslavs to bring about a final understanding and settlement.

QUESTION: I understand when you began the talks with Mr. Velebit in February 1954, they were held with the delegations from the three parties, each with a number of experts and advisers, and that this made it difficult to get to the meat of the negotiation because it seemed more like a formal and large-scale enterprise than a very quiet, personal one. Is this your recollection?

HARRISON: Well, it is a long time ago and I'm afraid I just cannot remember the circumstances of the first meeting. I remember perfectly the house in Harrington Gardens in London where we met with Velebit, and my recollection is that it was certainly pretty informal. That is certainly how it developed, but quite honestly I cannot remember precisely how the first meeting was held. Now that you mention it, I think I do remember that we did assemble with a number of advisers and helpers, and that it was rather formal with statements of prepared positions and that kind of thing. But my recollection is that after the formal statements of position were made, we very quickly went into much more informal discussions, where I suspect that we each had one helper present. Though I cannot remember this precisely, I think for quite a lot of the time I had one assistant present who took the notes and records and was generally an expert adviser as necessary.

QUESTION: If it came to a meeting among the three of you, each had one expert taking notes?

HARRISON: As far as I remember, but quite honestly, I cannot remember that. I think quite often we may have met *à trois*, but I am afraid I just cannot remember that point. Certainly we did come down to at the most, I think, two per side, and it may be that quite often we were only one per side.

QUESTION: Do you recall the extent of the Yugoslav claims or proposals in the beginning? Was there a progression from making rather extensive claims to a more reasonable position later on?

HARRISON: My recollection is that at the first formal statement of positions, Mr. Velebit put forth the Yugoslav claim for the whole Free Territory of Trieste. Tommy Thompson and I were obliged to remind him that, after all, we were seeking to reach a settlement and this was not going to get us anywhere. Mr. Velebit, who was very reasonable, quickly accepted this. I think he had to get his original position into the record. But thereafter we moved very quickly to a discussion of possibilities centering on the zonal boundary, and if I remember rightly, the first proposals were for modifications of the zonal boundary in terms of Yugoslav acquisitions in Zone A, and the surrender to the Italians of a triangle of territory on the Zone A-Yugoslav border. But that approach did not seem to be making much progress either, so I think fairly quickly we got down to a discussion of possible corrections of the zonal frontier involving really very small amounts of territory.

That was not the only element, of course, in the discussion. In addition to the territorial element, there was the free port of Trieste, and there was the protection of minorities. For approximately four months those were the things which we were discussing with Velebit, and which at the end of May we had reduced to a series of formulae which we thought we could reasonably take to the Italians.

QUESTION: On the territorial question, did you have the impression from the beginning that the Yugoslavs would settle on something like the zonal boundary if they couldn't get to the sea through the suburbs of Trieste as they had originally proposed; that they were going to accept the territorial status quo with some slight changes?

HARRISON: Yes, I think that was so, because with the break between Belgrade and Moscow in 1948, I think the Yugoslavs realized that their position was a good deal weaker than it had been before, and that they could no longer hope to obtain the major concessions which they had hoped to get in Zone A.

QUESTION: Were there real difficulties about the other points—about the minorities and the free port? Was that what most of the time was devoted to?

HARRISON: Yes, I think it was, but I don't think it was so much the difficulties as the sheer complexity of trying to work out and then agree on a statute which would cover the extremely complex ethnic, national, and social situation in the Free Territory. There were also, of course, quite a number of economic questions which had to be considered, such as compensation and the terms of a free port in Trieste for the Yugoslavs. So all these discussions were fairly technical and, in some cases, fairly complex, although I think we probably all felt that an ethnic statute—a minorities statute—was not really going to be tremendously effective in practice. So much of this exercise was in fact an exercise in window dressing, and whether it was on the territorial issue or on the minorities issue, what we had to do was to build up a very handsome, substantial facade, in order that both the Italian and Yugoslav governments could sell it to their people.

QUESTION: The Yugoslavs made quite a point, did they not, about the permanent nature of the settlement which was difficult for you to deal with?

BRITISH NEGOTIATOR

HARRISON: That is perfectly correct. The Yugoslavs wanted it to be a final settlement, but we knew that this would be quite unacceptable to the Italians; that any solution we took to the Italians which suggested that the solution would be final would not stand a chance of acceptance. So I think we did devise a formula in the end which worked, which was that the U.S. government and Her Majesty's government would not support any further claims by either side in the area, and this satisfied the Yugoslavs and was acceptable to the Italians. There were doors and windows left open for the future, of course, but no matter.

QUESTION: In a way they are still open. On the other hand, doesn't the number of years that this settlement has endured without a public demand for revision give an impression of permanence?

HARRISON: Yes, I think it stuck, insofar as anything sticks in international affairs for more than a certain period of years.

QUESTION: I suppose that was your calculation and it actually has worked out. Do you think it was a chance well worth taking?

HARRISON: Well, we reckoned, and I think correctly, that neither the Yugoslavs nor the Italians were in any position to enforce their claims by military action on their own—without support from elsewhere—and that that was unlikely to happen, not only because they were not in a position to do it, but because frankly at that time one of the basic elements in the situation was the desire, as it seemed to us, on both sides—in Belgrade and in Rome—to reach a settlement on this question. With that element of good will, one could take a chance, I think, on perpetuity.

QUESTION: This is perhaps a key to it. You mentioned in the beginning how difficult a task it was, without any assurance of success, because it had been a problem which had been unresolved for long. Nevertheless, do you think there was a mood on both sides that somehow this time it was in the interest of both to make a real effort for settlement and not to keep it open as a dangerous issue?

HARRISON: I am sure that is correct.

QUESTION: Was there also the fact, speaking of how permanent the settlement might be, that legally it would have been very difficult to make a permanent settlement, in view of the peace treaty and the requirement, presumably, that the Russians and others who were signatories to that peace treaty would have to be brought into it?

HARRISON: That is correct, but I think the Russians went on record in October 1954 in the United Nations as accepting this settlement. So with Russian acceptance—and the French, of course, accepted it as well; I don't know what the Chinese did—and with the four permanent members primarily concerned accepting the settlement, it had reasonable elements of perpetuity to it.

QUESTION: That's right. Legally, however, is there still a peace treaty which provides for a Free Territory of Trieste?

HARRISON: Well, I expect so. I cannot remember whether the peace treaty was ever modified. I suspect not.

QUESTION: Of course, it was in the hands of the Security Council for all practical purposes, and didn't the Security Council accept it, in fact, if not in law?

BRITISH NEGOTIATOR

HARRISON: But still, of course, the fact does remain that if there were a new government in Yugoslavia or Italy which felt that they really wanted to press their claims, they could do so. On the record both have maintained their claims for the whole Trieste territory, and I suppose they could legally, if we are talking entirely in legal terms, say that their positions had never been compromised on that.

QUESTION: Now, to turn to the way in which you handled the negotiation. Did you and Thompson work out a strategy of your own in dealing first with the Yugoslavs to reduce their claims, or did you merely reason with them as you talked with them, trying to modify their position to one which you felt the Italians could accept?

HARRISON: I think, as in all multilateral negotiations of this kind, Tommy Thompson and I as intermediaries frequently met before or after the meetings in order to consider where we went next, and, of course, both of us were in touch with our own governments as necessary on what was required. Certainly my Foreign Secretary, Anthony Eden, at the appropriate time intervened with Brosio and Velebit, and I have no doubt the same thing happened in Washington. But by and large we were left very much on our own to handle this negotiation. It was only if and when we felt that things were getting stuck and that a word would be helpful, that our foreign ministers intervened. I think it was accepted that Brosio and Velebit would do their utmost—they were men of great good will, courage, experience and wisdom—to try to narrow the issues, and pressure from government to government would not necessarily be helpful except at precisely the right moment. So Thompson and I did work out before each meeting how we would try to proceed, what we thought we could accept, where we would have to exert pressure for more concessions, and so on.

QUESTION: I recall from our conversation with him that he [Thompson] felt that the Department of State did not really give him realistic instructions; that he had to take a good deal of initiative and convince them as he was going along that he was doing what had to be done. Did you have any problem like that?

HARRISON: Well, as I said in the beginning, this undertaking was regarded very much as a forlorn hope when we began. No one really thought that we were going to get anywhere at all. So for a long period of time, probably three months anyway, no one in higher authority took any great interest in what I was doing. I reported to my permanent Undersecretary, [Sir] Ivone Kirkpatrick, as things went along, and it was only at a much later stage, when we had something to put to the Italians, that the Foreign Secretary really took a personal interest.

QUESTION: Did you and Thompson generally have harmony in your approach to your task? Were there any times when you disagreed with each other?

HARRISON: To the best of my recollection, there was never any disagreement on our approach to this. I just cannot remember any.

QUESTION: Of course, it was a situation in which there was no basic disagreement between the two governments on the question. Both wanted to get it settled. Do you suppose there was any conflict of interest that might have brought about difficulties?

HARRISON: There was absolutely no conflict of interest. I think, looking back now, perhaps the only slight nuance of difference was that for various reasons I think probably the U.S. government was slightly more sensitive about the Italian situation than we were.

BRITISH NEGOTIATOR

QUESTION: Was that because of the question of the European Defense Community?

HARRISON: Because of the E.D.C., and possibly—is there an Italian lobby in Washington? I do not know.

QUESTION: Well, there always is, but on the Trieste question I do not recall its being vocal at the time.

HARRISON: I think there was a slightly softer feeling in Washington for Italian sensibilities, because, after all, the Italian situation was far more tricky internally than the Yugoslav situation.

QUESTION: Yes, as I recall there were two or three changes of government within a couple of months at the beginning of 1954. Is that your recollection?

HARRISON: Yes.

QUESTION: Let us turn for a moment to the question of secrecy. You mentioned that secrecy worked pretty well in this case. There was no publicity about the negotiations and other governments were not informed, I gather. I should like to get your judgment on the importance of secrecy in this kind of negotiation. Could it have been done in any other way? Was this one of the vital factors determining success with the two parties, particularly in view of the plan of negotiating with one first, and then the other?

HARRISON: I have no doubt at all that secrecy was the absolute essence of the success of the negotiation. The French, of course, knew we were carrying on these talks. The Italian and Yugoslav governments knew, as well as the American and British governments, and that was, so far as I remember, absolutely all. There were no press leaks of any kind.

We deliberately first met in the Yugoslav embassy and then in the Italian embassy, so that there would be no risk. I forget how far Tommy must have been incognito in some ways. Otherwise it would have been a bit obvious that something was up—the Ambassador to Vienna being there. But confidentiality was maintained right through to the end, and I am sure that it was that which enabled us to carry the negotiation through. It was particularly important, I think, for the Italians and Yugoslavs, because if the Italian and Yugoslav governments had been under public pressure, as they certainly would have been from the independentists, the nationalists, the Slovenes, and all the rest of them, I think that the negotiation would never have got off the ground at all.

QUESTION: One of the difficulties was keeping from the Italians what you were discussing with the Yugoslavs, wasn't it? To what extent were they informed and involved? I gather they had some worries that they were not getting the whole story?

HARRISON: We kept the French regularly informed, but I do not remember if we told the Italians how things were going for those four months from February until the end of May when we went to Brosio. If I remember rightly, they had their own domestic problems at that time. I think the Pella government [Giuseppe Pella, Italian Prime Minister for a six-month period, 1953–1954] fell in January and Scelba came in February. I think they had quite a lot of domestic problems then, and Scelba, in particular, was much less deeply concerned with Trieste than De Gasperi [Alcide de Gasperi, Italian Prime Minister, 1946–1953] or Pella had been. So, although I would not like to be dogmatic about this, I do not remember our keeping the Italians informed about the negotiations with Velebit. I think it was simply left that when we had something which we felt we could put to them, we would. And whether we told them from time to time that things were moving, I am afraid I cannot remember.

QUESTION: According to the account which J. B. Duroselle wrote of these developments—he had access to some official papers in the Italian archives—there were complaints from the Italians that their British and American friends were not telling them what was going on. Is that your recollection?

HARRISON: That is my recollection, yes.

QUESTION: Did the French ever express any views on this themselves? You mention that they were quite willing to be outside of the negotiations and not participate. Were they informed to some degree?

HARRISON: Yes, my recollection is that I saw Claude Lebel [French Counselor of Embassy in London] regularly here in London, and he reported back to the Quai. But I think the French had their own problems at that time, and we certainly were never pressed to say more than we wanted to.

QUESTION: Suppose we look at the Yugoslavs' position as they developed it, as it softened over the course of the talks in four months. Do you think this had something to do with their need for economic and military aid which was evident at that time? Were they in any sense under pressure at the negotiating table, even if they did not admit it, to come to an agreement with you because of that situation?

HARRISON: I think that by October 1954 their international position was improving, because Stalin had died, and there was some degree of rapprochement with the Soviet Union. So that internationally they were not as isolated as they had been. But I think they had had a very bad harvest, if I remember rightly, and they certainly were looking forward to help both in finance and and in goods as part of the quid pro quo for concessions in the Free Territory.

QUESTION: Of course, we had a joint American-British-French aid program that we first worked out in 1951 and went on over a period of three years. I think it was 1953 or 1954 before the special tripartite arrangements came to an end. There was never any condition put on the extension of that aid to the effect that we were looking for a more conciliatory attitude on Trieste, or anything of that kind. On the other hand, I think the volume of aid had gone down. British aid had dropped and I think was going to be terminated very soon because of your own economic situation, and that must have been in the background. The Yugoslavs were still in a difficult position, experiencing droughts every other year, 1950, 1952, and 1954 each with bad harvests. So that it is conceivable that they did not want to lose an opportunity to reach an agreement which they knew we wanted very much, because of the effect it might have had on their aid program. On the other hand, it is difficult to find any specific reference to it. Did you discuss it at all with them?

HARRISON: We certainly did not discuss it. The Yugoslavs being a proud people, even if it were at the back of their minds, I doubt whether it was a major factor in their making the concessions which they did. I think that the incentive of $30 million to build a port at Koper, if I remember rightly, and the two million pounds which we offered, were more influential than the fear that if they were not helpful, it might have had an effect on aid generally.

QUESTION: Yes, I imagine that's right. Maybe the negotiation was helped along a little by the prospect of specific aid directed toward construction needs which would grow out of the agreement?

HARRISON: I really think so.

QUESTION: You mentioned Yugoslavia's relations with the Soviet Union. It is very difficult to fix a time when they began to feel more at ease about their relations with the Soviet Union, but it is interesting that the Balkan Alliance with Greece and Turkey which they negotiated at this time—I think it was concluded in August—and represented the high point of their military collaboration with the West, such as it was, almost immediately fell into disuse and was rarely mentioned by them thereafter because of the new relation with the Soviet Union. Nevertheless, they did not go back on the agreement on Trieste they had made in May, and Tito finally sealed it in September with Robert Murphy. It was about this time in the fall of 1954, I think, in October or November, that there were open signs that there was a new attitude in both Belgrade and Moscow, on possibilities of coexistence rather than cold war between them.

HARRISON: Yes, but I think that with the death of Stalin, they already had a feeling, especially with Malenkov [Georgi Malenkov, Soviet Premier, 1953–1956] coming in, that things were going to be easier.

QUESTION: Yes, one would like to have more information on how that change developed. Once they began to digest the fact that it was a different Soviet Union, at least a different leadership, following Stalin's death, the question how long it took to find any concrete effect of it in the Soviet-Yugoslav relationship is one to which I suppose we will not have an adequate answer until we get more revelations from the Yugoslav side.

HARRISON: I think the main external pressure on the

Yugoslavs in the Trieste matter was really the fact that they realized that we, the British and the Americans, could at any time hand over Zone A to the Italians, leaving Italian claims on Zone B not only wide open, but also open to possible support from Washington and London, and they knew they were not really going to get anything out of Zone A. So taking a realistic view of it, against the general context of wanting to live in reasonable amity with a neighbor, they came to the conclusion that they had really better settle.

QUESTION: Now, once you had the agreement at the end of May with Velebit did you know you had something which had a pretty good chance of acceptance by Italy?

HARRISON: Yes, we did. We put the terms which we had agreed to with Velebit to Brosio, on June 1, I think it was, covering the territorial terms, the terms for protection of minorities in Trieste, and other matters. I think that we did actually feel, quite apart from the fact that the terms were not unreasonable, that in Scelba we had someone who was not obsessed with Trieste in the same way as his two predecessors. De Gasperi just could not be shaken free of the tripartite proposal of 1948. Pella, of course, was quite a sword brandisher, whereas Scelba was much more relaxed about it all.

Right from the beginning we felt that Brosio was ready to agree that this was something that could be put to his government—although in the first place, of course, he had to remind us that Italian claims were originally for the whole of the Free Territory and were endorsed by the tripartite proposal; that they later were ready to take what was proposed in the decision of October 8, 1953; and that what the Italian government was now being asked to accept was something even less than that.

But if I remember rightly, after the first meeting, I think he took it really without demur. He did not show signs of total disgruntlement with the suggested terms.

QUESTION: Did he tell you he was going to have a very difficult time with his own government?

HARRISON: Oh, he may well have said so. It would be the natural thing to say at the beginning of a tough negotiation. I think he almost certainly did say that, and I think it was perfectly true as well. I believe that he did have a very difficult time and that he showed immense courage in pressing some of these terms on his government.

QUESTION: There was a great deal of discussion in this next stage about the boundary, all very slight in terms of the size of the territories involved, but nevertheless argued with some vigor. Did you have the impression that this was very important to them? Did they need some territory in Zone B just to show there was an exchange?

HARRISON: Yes, I am quite certain that was so; that this territorial thing really did matter from the point of view of presentation. As I said earlier, for both Belgrade and Rome presentation was a very important element. But aren't we jumping now to the fourth stage, which was where Thompson and I became true intermediaries? We have not reached that stage yet.

QUESTION: Right. Is there anything you recall of the third stage—that is, of the attempt to persuade the Italians of the general acceptability of the agreement reached with the Yugoslavs. Was there bound to be something left over for the fourth stage, because they could not accept the agreement without some amendment? Was it merely a question of saving their own dignity as they saw it?

GEOFFREY W. HARRISON

HARRISON: I remember it but not in detail. I think we reached the stage where we became intermediaries on July 14, so that leaves about six weeks while we were conferring with the Italians. And I recall that there was a lot of to-ing and fro-ing about territorial claims. There were places like Lazzaretto and Muggia about which we spent an inordinate time talking—little communities of a few hundred souls, and a few square miles, really. I suppose we did all that, but it hasn't really left much of an impression on my mind.

QUESTION: As I recall from the record, the Italians were not really enthusiastic about some rather useless territory from Zone B that the Yugoslavs had offered, the triangle you mentioned. Is that right?

HARRISON: Certainly.

QUESTION: But they did want to go down the coast a bit to get some Italian fishing villages and communications there, and more breathing space around the port of Trieste. The Yugoslavs were reluctant to accept that. Is this where there was a deadlock?

HARRISON: Yes, that is why I say it moved right into the fourth stage here, because this was where we really got down to the argument about Punta Sottile, which was approximately two square miles, and on which the whole thing nearly foundered at one point. I mean, that is what we finally were arguing about. I cannot remember if there was any serious argument about the statute for minorities or indeed about the free port. I think those were fairly acceptable, because ultimately it came down to the presentation in terms of territorial concessions.

QUESTION: Even though this created a deadlock, there was no real fear on your part that the Italians would break off at any time?

HARRISON: No, I do not think there was a fear of that, but there did come a point in time when Anthony Eden did ask Brosio—I think about the end of July, perhaps in August—to go back to Rome and really put all possible pressure on his government to settle the territorial question. Again, it did not actually get things moving. If I go on perhaps to the next stage, I think what really broke the log jam was when Murphy came into the picture.

QUESTION: Was his mission a suggestion from the U.S. side that maybe the old acquaintance between Murphy and Tito might help at this stage?

HARRISON: I am sure that was so. I mean, I do not think we would have suggested it. I cannot remember how it came up. But certainly we were very glad to have the suggestion. If I remember rightly, it was September 14 when Murphy went to Belgrade, and it was at that point that the log jam was broken. It was broken perhaps primarily because an offer of wheat came at some point, either just before or at the time of the mission. It was the fact that he was able to fly on to Rome with two alternative suggestions on territory, giving the Italians the possibility of choosing one or the other, which I think just turned the corner for us. They accepted one of the two alternatives, and after that we were home and dry.

QUESTION: We got the impression from Velebit that Tito really did not care about a few square miles of territory; that what he wanted was the agreement, and that he was immensely pleased that Murphy came with a personal letter from President Eisenhower. Is that your interpretation?

HARRISON: Exactly that, yes.

GEOFFREY W. HARRISON

QUESTION: Showing that Yugoslavia was not being in any way put upon, with a forced solution or anything like that?

HARRISON: Of course, there was so much of that. I think that is why we had to tread so carefully on both sides, because the *diktat* had been tried, and the Yugoslavs in their time had felt rather neglected: 1948, 1953 in October, and so on. I think that with people like the Yugoslavs, that gesture was greatly appreciated, and I think it paid off very well indeed.

QUESTION: It seems to me in retrospect that the two governments took such care at this time not to appear to be forcing anything on the Yugoslavs on behalf of Italy, that it might have had some reaction on the Italian side. After all the Italians were the ally—they were in the Western camp and so forth—and Yugoslavia was not. Did the Italians try to play on this Western tie?

HARRISON: Oh, yes. They never stopped playing on that tie from 1945 onwards. They certainly played on it, but not beyond reason, I don't think. After all, this really was a very gentlemanly negotiation. And although these things were brought up, they were brought up in a sensitive way because Velebit and Brosio were very sensitive people in those terms. It was a very ideal diplomatic negotiation. We all respected each other's sensibilities and interests, and so on. Although all the notes and chords were struck, it was done in such a way that they did not have to be thumped. I mean, we all appreciated what was involved throughout.

QUESTION: We might now consider a more general question to see how this rather narrow negotiation on a small territorial question fits into the European political situation of that time. I am thinking particularly of

Yugoslavia's position with respect to the West and the Soviet Union, but also of relations among the Western allies, and the question of the European Defense Community, which was then up for ratification before several parliaments of the European NATO countries.

There was also the rather curious episode of Yugoslavia's alliance, then under negotiation, with Greece and Turkey, in which it was sometimes stated that Italy might become a member of that alliance in due course. And finally, certain ideas were held in the West concerning closer cooperation with Yugoslavia—ideas which eventually did not develop into practice because the Yugoslavs were able to find a new relationship with the Soviet Union, enabling them to get back to a more strictly nonaligned position in which they were no longer talking about military cooperation with the West. Do you have any comments on the political context in which the Trieste settlement took place?

HARRISON: Yes. I think one certainly has to take the Trieste negotiation in the context not only of the current European situation, but in the context of actions taken and statements made over the previous seven years or so. Undoubtedly in the early stages, especially those culminating in the tripartite proposal of 1948, it was the fact that Yugoslavia was on closer terms with the Soviet Union that made the British and American governments lean fairly heavily toward the Italians. I think the idea that the communists—Belgrade linked with Moscow—should encroach right down to the Adriatic, not only through Zone B but through Zone A as well, was one which caused considerable alarm in the West. With the break in 1948 between Belgrade and Moscow, of course, the situation changed a little bit, in that the possibility of drawing Tito—Yugoslavia—away from the Eastern bloc was extremely attractive. And as that possibility grew more attractive, the position of the Italians grew slightly weaker, so that then one had variations in the way in which Washington and London treated the Trieste situation.

One thing which the Italians were always able to play on was their friendship with the Western powers. They were very much in the Western camp. And also, whatever weakness they had they could play in order to prod us into action, because they could continually come along and say, "Well, unless something is done in our favor in Trieste, we can lose the election." That card was played two or three times, and it almost always took a trick; I think I'm right in saying that various stages of participation of the Italians in Allied military government in Zone A were brought about by threats that unless they had something of this sort, they were going to be in trouble in their elections.

There was also the question of the E.D.C., which, as you say, was up for ratification. It was relevant both to the French and to the Italians, but particularly to the Italians. This was something which carried a greater weight in Washington than even in London. And as I said earlier, I think that Washington, partly for that reason, always was a little bit more inclined than London to lean toward the Italian side.

QUESTION: You mentioned before the Italian internal situation. Is there anything further that comes to mind about that, other than that there was continuing pressure, because of their saying that the Christian Democratic party depended on a position which took account of their interest in Trieste in order to win elections. Did they argue that they couldn't afford to allow any settlement which they could not defend within the country, or else their electoral position would be irreparably damaged? Did this change when the Scelba government came into power?

HARRISON: Of course, you remember that in 1947 to 1948 we were extremely concerned about the internal political situations both in France and in Italy, because the communist parties were getting up to 30, 35, 40 percent in elections. At that time I was in Moscow, and it looked as though the Russians were hoping for and putting all their money on a revolution by democratic means in France and Italy, which could bring the communists into power constitutionally in those two countries. And after all, although the real risk had passed by February or March 1948, I think basically the situation was still pretty uncertain, with a very large communist minority in both countries. We are talking about Italy primarily. So it was always a matter of major concern to insure that a Christian Democrat government did hold the balance of power there. So that when De Gasperi or Pella came to us and said that, "Unless you help us with Trieste, we shall be in trouble; we may lose the election," it was always a very powerful weapon.

By 1954, I think the situation was more stable, Scelba seemed to handle it differently, anyway. Trieste was much less a factor of electoral politics, I think, by then, and indeed far less an element in Italian foreign policy.

QUESTION: What was your estimate as to how the Italians weighed the possibility of refusing to go along with the agreement? You said before that they expected a settlement roughly on zonal lines, something which they could accept. They got something a little worse in the territorial sense, but at the same time you said that, in your judgment, they really did not give you the impression that they would turn it down.

HARRISON: No, I do not remember that I ever had the feeling that they were going to turn it down out of hand. As I say, in August and September we were stuck on this wretched little two square miles in the Punta Sottile area and it did seem rather uncertain.

QUESTION: Did you feel that they might make the decision not to accept?

HARRISON: I do not think we really felt that at any point. As I said, things did seem to have got stuck by the end of August or so, but there were still a number of strings to our bow. I do not think that we really felt that we had come to the end of the road then. And in fact, of course, Murphy was one of the strings, and he was effective in breaking the log jam. Within a fortnight of his visits to Belgrade and to Rome, we got the whole thing tied up.

QUESTION: This raises the question whether at any time the U.S. or the U.K. stepped out of the purely mediatory role and took a position of trying rather strongly to persuade the Italians to accept—this being the best deal that they could possibly get and a chance that should not be ignored?

HARRISON: Oh yes, I think there certainly came a point when we both did that. As I said, Anthony Eden did ask Brosio probably in early August, somewhere thereabouts, to go back to Rome in order to urge his government to accept the proposals, and I suppose essentially America's policy was very much to press for a settlement.

I think our intermediary role finished when we had reduced the differences between the two governments—between the Italians and Yugoslavs—to that two square miles of territory. I think after that point we stepped out of our intermediary role, and started using such persuasion—I do not say pressure—as was available to us to try to clinch the matter.

QUESTION: That is an interesting point. Compared with other negotiations where you have a purely good offices or mediation role played by a third party, in this case the two powers went beyond being mediators, beyond merely explaining one side's views to the other and attempting to make them more likely to agree. They also happened to be the two powers which were legally in Zone A as occupying powers with their military forces there. They were in different relationships with the two parties—one an ally, the other a helper and good friend—but had influence with both. Do you agree it was a rather unique situation in which we found ourselves and played on all those aspects of it in order to pull it off?

HARRISON: That is certainly so. I think I would say that at no stage were we simply a postbox. We were always considerably more active than that.

QUESTION: We have already mentioned the Murphy mission. Did Murphy speak on behalf of the U.S. government or the two governments?

HARRISON: On behalf of the U.S. government, I think. Yes, this was an American initiative.

QUESTION: Now I want to ask you some questions before proceeding to some general considerations. Do any other points occur to you with respect to the negotiation itself and what it accomplished? One thing that strikes me is the remarkable success, looking back on it now nearly twenty years later. Not only did it pretty much put a seal on the territorial settlement, which has not been disturbed even with words very much since that time, but also everything else has worked out in the Italian-Yugoslav relationship. Look at the tremendous daily traffic across the borders, intensive trade between the two countries, and in general a relationship which is far removed from what it had been before the agreement. Perhaps it is not a proper question to ask, but did you have any idea of the accomplishments that this particular agreement would bring about when you were doing it?

HARRISON: I think we certainly hoped it, and perhaps to some extent we may have sensed it, because one of the absolutely essential ingredients of the success of the negotiation was the fact that there was, as it seemed to us, a very real desire on the part of both Belgrade and Rome to get this issue settled, so that the two neighbors across the Adriatic could proceed to a much more fruitful and constructive relationship than they had had before. Unless they had had that desire, there would have been no settlement. But as they had that desire and a settlement was achieved, I think it was reasonable to hope that it would fructify, as indeed it has.

QUESTION: When you look at April 1948, with the tripartite offer of the whole of the Free Territory to Italy, and again at the October 1953 declaration, it is apparent that the two parties simply were not ready at those times for the kind of agreement which you finally got at the end of 1954. I suppose that is the story about almost any negotiation—namely, that there has to be a general readiness; the time has to be ripe. Both governments have to be ready to see that there are benefits to be gained by an agreement that is not wholly satisfactory to them, as opposed to the benefits of the situation that results if they refuse to negotiate. Somehow in terms of the way the historical development took place this seemed to be the time, the way, and the right people. In some ways things came together at the right time. Do you agree?

BRITISH NEGOTIATOR

HARRISON: Yes. That is precisely the way I see it. First of all, I think that there had to be a catalyst to precipitate the realization on the part both of the Italians and the Yugoslavs that unless something was done, the situation was going to get a lot worse and the two countries could find themselves in active military hostilities. And I think one can say that the October 8 decision to impose a unilateral settlement was a catalyst.

Now, that decision caused a great deal of resentment in the first place in Yugoslavia and afterwards in Italy, but it also caused quite a pother here in Parliament, and so far as I know in the States as well. There certainly was quite strong criticism here in Parliament of the ineptness—if I remember rightly what Dalton [Hugh Dalton, Labor party member] called it—or incompetence of the diplomatic technique employed, and so on. In his memoirs Anthony Eden says that he never regretted having done this because he thought it was what really set things going, and I think he makes the remark that peace in fact never comes of itself. One has to take risks in achieving peace. I think those are his concluding words in his chapter on the Trieste negotiation.

So first of all, I think, although I would not say you had to have it, the fact of the October 8 decision was a precipitating factor which brought home both to Rome and Belgrade that unless something was done, there would be real dangers in the situation.

Second, I think that in both countries there was a very real feeling that they had common interests, and that they had much better try and get this question out of the way; that by and large there was virtually no room to maneuver on either side. They both claimed to have rights to more territory. They both knew they could not get it. They both realized that the best they could hope to get was Zone A and Zone B, respectively. So they decided with reason and logic, I think, they had better make the best of it and get a settlement.

It so happened that the time was ripe, and ripeness of time is one of the absolute essences of diplomacy. It is never doing the right thing at the wrong time, or the wrong thing at the right time for that matter. You have to do the right thing at the right time, and it so happens that the *Stimmung*, as the Germans would say, was right for this negotiation. So, in short, the circumstances were such that it was possible, provided the situation was handled properly, to get a settlement of this question.

QUESTION: Yes, it could have been mishandled as in times gone by, but it wasn't.

HARRISON: Of course on that point, the handling of it, perhaps I might say that I think there were three other ingredients. One was that basically we were not hurried. After all, we took nine months. And the fact that no one was treading on our tails all the time saying, "Hurry, hurry up, hurry up, get a decision, get a settlement," I think made absolutely all the difference, because we could take it at our own pace, and we did not appear to be pressurizing either side. Fortunately both in Yugoslavia and in Italy for various reasons there were no internal pressures to get the thing settled. And linked with that was the fact that the negotiations were secret and therefore pressures were not being generated either in those countries or elsewhere to find out what was happening, how it was going, who was conceding what, and all the rest of it. So that I think the facts that we had the time and we were operating in secrecy meant that the full element of patience in working on problems and trying to find an answer acceptable to both sides, both in substance and in presentation, worked to good advantage. We had the time to do it.

There is just one other element which I do think

should be mentioned, and that was that both Velebit and Brosio were rather remarkable people. We were lucky that we had two people like that as the main protagonists, because they were very experienced people, not only in diplomacy but generally. They had great wisdom, patience, and above all, I think, courage, because this was an explosive issue, and it did need courage both for Velebit and for Brosio to keep going back to their governments saying, "I'm sorry, I can't get that; I can't get this; I have to give this away," and so on. And they did it. They never boggled in any way. They went back; they saw their chiefs; and eventually they got the agreement. But I thought it was courage of a high order on the part of both.

QUESTION: Yes. I think that is a very good statement which takes account of much of what I was still going to ask you. Of course, there were so many unique things in this particular exercise in diplomacy. You do not find anything comparable, do you, in other experiences of your own diplomatic career?

HARRISON: Well, no. Anthony Eden was always saying after that, time and time again, "Why can't we settle Cyprus? Why can't we settle the Arab-Israeli conflict along the same lines as the Trieste negotiations?" He did feel that it was a classic example of how a diplomatic issue of this kind could be settled. Of course the answer is that these circumstances in fact never repeat themselves, either in terms of timing or circumstances or anything else, in the case of other problems. There were the various factors I listed which I think made the Trieste settlement possible, but they have never, unfortunately, been available for Cyprus or Israel.

QUESTION: I think it was a bit deceptive in that way. Mr. Dulles—this may have been the one thing he agreed with Anthony Eden on—wanted to apply it to the Middle East, and, as you may recall, they each named a diplomat to play the same role as you and Thompson played and draw up some draft treaties and other settlements which they might present separately to Egypt and Israel. As you know, it all came to nothing, but Trieste was always cited as a way some things could be done.

HARRISON: I think a nearer parallel really is Cyprus, and I would not despair that one day Cyprus might be settled in that way, for it is a far more comparable problem than the Arab-Israel dispute, which is too big, too fundamental.

QUESTION: Well, possibly so. Of course there are three parties there instead of two. Let me ask you just one last question about the Soviets. The Soviet Union was always in the background, wasn't it? This was a time of much concern with the position of the Soviet Union. The year began with the conference in Berlin, then came the Geneva conference and the E.D.C. affair. One of the surprising things to me is that the Russians really had no role in this Trieste settlement at all. Do you agree?

HARRISON: The Russians never really came into the picture. Once we had eliminated them in October 1953 they really never entered our calculations again.

QUESTION: This was, of course, largely the outcome of what happened in 1948. So long as Yugoslavia was not in any way a surrogate for Soviet ambition or policies, we had a chance to do this without worrying too much about how the Russians might try to intervene and profit by it.

HARRISON: That is certainly true. They also had their hands full at home at that time.

CHAPTER THREE

The Yugoslav Negotiator, Vladimir Velebit

In this interview with Joseph E. Johnson and John C. Campbell, which took place in the offices of the Academy for Educational Development in New York City in January 1972, Vladimir Velebit outlines the evolution of the dispute through centuries of history and two world wars. His contribution is notable for its sense of the dynamics of history which has infused the attitudes of Yugoslavs. At the same time he is utterly realistic in his assessment of how cold-war politics determined both the critical decisions of 1945 and the ultimate settlement in 1954. His insider's vantage point allows a first-hand look at how Yugoslavia stood poised between East and West.

Velebit shows why the time was right for settlement, and the reasons why his government found it advantageous to agree. His account illustrates how governments are sometimes forced to assume certain negotiating stances, and what elements are necessary to move them from these positions. His own assessment of the London talks is candid and keen, in many respects a unique and indispensable contribution.

A participant in the National Liberation movement during World War II, Velebit served in Marshal Tito's government during and after the war. He organized, practically from scratch, the new Ministry of Foreign Affairs. He undertook important negotiations with the Soviet Union before the break with Stalin in 1948—his name, incidentally, figured prominently in the Soviet charges against Yugoslavia in that year—and had a key role in developing new relationships with the Western powers. He served briefly, and uncomfortably, as Yugoslavia's Ambassador in Rome in the early 1950s.

During the 1954 Trieste negotiations, Velebit was Ambassador to Great Britain, and his private residence in London served as the locale for the bulk of conversations with Thompson and Harrison. The agreement of 1954 provided the capstone to his diplomatic career, even though personally he was never reconciled to Yugoslavia's failure to get Trieste. From 1960 until 1967 he left his government's employ to serve the international community as Executive Secretary of the United Nations Commission for Europe located in Geneva. He now resides in Yugoslavia.

QUESTION: Near the end of December 1953, just before your talks began in London, how did the dispute about Trieste fall into the general picture of Yugoslavia's position in the world as it looked both to the West and to the East? We would like to get the question of Trieste in the context of a general foreign policy position at that time.

VELEBIT: Trieste was one of the most important problems—national, ethnic, and political—for my country. You know that Yugoslavia is a federal republic composed of several national republics and one of these is the Republic of Slovenia. The Slovenes are the most developed, the most civilized, if I may say so, of all the Yugoslav republics, and they have been squeezed for nearly one thousand years between two big nations—the Germans in the north and the Italians in the west. From the north the process of Germanization and slow repression of the Slovenes went on for almost a thousand years. On the western side, the Italians, if you remember history, were not a compact and organized state at that time. They were in that period divided into a lot of small towns and republics that of course could not exert strong pressure against the Slovenes as the Germans did. The ethnic frontier between the Italian elements and the Slavic elements has remained practically unchanged from the coming of Slavs to Europe. This ethnic frontier runs roughly along the flow of the River Soča (Isonzo).

Of course, the Venetians in their heyday pursued a policy of domination of the Adriatic Sea, and for this reason they established a number of colonies in Istria and along the Dalmatian coast. In some periods they were able to encroach on a little more territory and to penetrate a little deeper, and often they were pushed back. I think we can say quite truly that they established permanent power in the northern part of the Adriatic, particularly on the coast of the Istrian peninsula, where they had a few very important strongholds or colonies.

I'm saying that in order to underline that Trieste in that period—three or four hundred years ago—was not really an important place at all. It was a fishing village inhabited by a mixture of Slovene fishermen and maybe some Venetian fishermen. But then the situation developed so that the lingua franca in the whole northern part of the Adriatic became Italian. The Italian language was used by the skippers, by the fishermen, by the sailors, and so on, and it was more or less required that if you chose the career of sailor, you had to learn some Italian.

It was the establishment of Austria in this area that changed the situation, for the Austrians chose the Bay of Trieste to develop the principal port of their empire.

And so Trieste had a very rapid development, and became quite an important European port.

As in most ports, the people of Trieste were of many nationalities. There were Greeks, Italians, Croats, Slovenes, Germans, and others, and all these formed an amalgamate which found employment in this thriving port and commercial city. The language in the city was prevalently Italian for the reasons which I tried to explain.

In the process of a town's growth, there is always a strong influx of landless peasants and the poor people from the surrounding areas. The surrounding villages of Trieste are one hundred percent Slovene; thirty or forty years ago, if you went two miles from the center of Trieste in any direction you could not find a nationality other than Slovene. Quite naturally these poor peasants from a limestone desert area looked for work in Trieste. The people who settled in Trieste were relatively quickly Italianized, because Trieste was a town of Italian language and Italian schools, and for employment on ships and in trade you had to speak the language. This process was particularly pronounced in the eighteenth century.

In the nineteenth century there was a change, because the Slovenes slowly began to develop their own bourgeoisie, and since Trieste was the center of this new social development, Slovene lawyers, doctors, craftsmen, and commercial tradesmen settled there. They were not willing, like the illiterate peasants who came earlier to Trieste, to abandon their language, culture, and Slovene civilization. They banded together and organized a number of associations, schools, cultural groups, and such, and they formed the nucleus of a constant Slovene population in Trieste.

From about 1860 to the 1900s, we had this very interesting phenomenon: the Italian population in Trieste was stagnant and the Slovene population was increasing rapidly, because all newcomers to Trieste were not denationalized as before, but found a way to include themselves in the existing Slovene community and preserve their nationality.

This process would have made Trieste, probably in fifty years, a town with a large Slovene majority. But two things prevented this. The first was the Austrian hostility against the Slavs, which with their rapid rate of growth were really the majority in the Austro-Hungarian Empire. For fear the Slavs would one day tear the empire apart, whenever they could the Austrian authorities gave preference to other ethnic groups. The Austrians did that, not only in the northern part of the Adriatic, but also on the whole Dalmatian coast down to the Albanian frontier. In all fairness I have to say they did not discriminate too harshly, because after all they considered the Germans the ruling group and all the other ethnic groups inferior to them, including the Italians. If they had to choose a preference they preferred the Italians to the Slovenes or to the Croats.

The second decisive factor was World War I. Of course the Italians wanted to cash in the prize which was promised to them for entering the war. If you remember the London agreement, then you know the British and French were extremely generous in giving away land that did not belong to them. So Yugoslavia was really just an infant born out of the circumstances and had no possibility to defend itself. So another large portion of ethnically Slav territory was given to the Italians in this period.

For me, that is of lesser importance. For me the question of greater importance is, why did the Italians push so hard to get a foothold in the Balkans? One of their policies was to have bridgeheads in the Balkans in order to pursue their imperialist policy there. The imperialist policy of the Italians was, I think, quite clearly demonstrated. They fought against the Turks in 1911. You know of their efforts to encroach on Greek territory as much as possible, culminating in the aggression of Mussolini against Greece in 1940. These were all signs that Italy, which was becoming a rather strong, industrially developed, expansive country, was looking for a region where it could expand its commercial and imperial interests. The Italians had to be rather careful to pick areas where they thought they would meet weak opponents, and these were the splinter countries in the Balkans. For this reason after World War I they wanted, of course, to have Istria and they got it; also Zadar (Zara), which is in the middle of Dalmatia. It was absolutely absurd to give to another country such an enclave, which has only, I think, about a hundred square kilometers of territory. They also got the islands of Lastovo (Lagosta) in the south, and thus practically dominated the whole Yugoslav coast.

This is an introduction to show that we South Slavs considered the real ethnic boundary to be as it had remained practically unchanged for about a thousand years, on the River Soča. And any encroachment from one side or the other side could and should be considered as a thorn in the body of the other ethnic unit.

As far as the economic element is concerned, Trieste was developed as the principal port of the Austro-Hungarian Empire. Any port needs a hinterland. Without it a port is useless, and Trieste, of course, for the Italians had no hinterland whatsoever. Trieste can of course serve a vast hinterland consisting of today's Austria, Hungary, and the whole northwestern part of Yugoslavia. Without it Trieste loses its role as a port. Trieste can be, of course, a pleasure resort. It can be an artificial industrial town because it has no raw material, and that is what the Americans and the British tried to make of it when they thought it was necessary for political reasons to give Trieste to the Italians. But the role of Trieste as a port is finished the moment Trieste is not part and parcel of Yugoslavia.

This was, I think, one of our main arguments in our dealings about Trieste, and furthermore we thought that we—the Yugoslavs—needed an efficient port for our trade operations. Why should we invest a lot of capital in building a new port when there was already a port in existence which had all the advantages necessary for our foreign trade?

QUESTION: May I specify a question to follow that? I assume that the Yugoslavs felt in 1945 and 1946, when the peace treaty negotiations were going on, that they had a chance to get Trieste—at least they certainly continued to include it in their claims—and they had Soviet support up to a certain point, though they did not have American, British, or French support. The Soviets eventually felt it was better, in order to break the log jam on the treaty, to agree to set up the Free Territory so that Yugoslavia did not get the port of Trieste at that time, but the Italians did not get it either. The compromise at least enabled the two countries to sign a peace treaty as soon as possible. When did the Yugoslav government come to accept the idea that maybe they were not going to get the city of Trieste?

You will recall the declaration of March 1948 when, in effect, the Americans, British and French said that the whole Free Territory should go to Italy, and there was tremendous protest on the Yugoslav side. And then in October 1953 the Americans and British made the proposal to turn over the governing authority and administration of Zone A to the Italians, which would be in effect a split of the territory along the zonal boundary. This proposal brought on great Yugoslav protests and demonstrations against the Americans and British. Then within three or four months of that crisis, serious negotiations began in London in order to reach a settlement which Yugoslavia and Italy could accept. Could you say something about the Yugoslav position at the time of that October 1953 crisis—whether the tremendous opposition, popular and governmental, was because of the prospect of losing the city and having the Italians there, or was it rather because Yugoslavia was not consulted and the proposal looked like a *diktat*?

I think this question is relevant to the ways in which all the governments concerned looked at the beginning of the negotiation in 1954. It is relevant to what the Yugoslav government's position and attitudes were, and to its thoughts about the possibility of a settlement, in view of what had happened in October. In this connection, Duroselle's study reads as follows: "If Pella's desire in bringing on the crisis had been to obtain quickly the entry of Italian troops into Zone A, the Anglo-American decision of October 8, 1953, had appeared to give him satisfaction. But the immediate and violent Yugoslav reaction should have wrecked that hope. If on the contrary he had only been searching to get movement started again in a situation that had been stuck in the mud, the result was perfectly attained."

VELEBIT: May I answer you again by going back a little? We were convinced that we had lost Trieste in 1945.

We knew we had lost Trieste when the British got American support to drive us out of the town. That was really the dramatic moment for us. We had suffered twelve thousand casualties in the surroundings of Trieste and in Trieste itself in order to be there first, because we thought—and I am still of that conviction—that whoever is in the possession of a certain territory has a ninety-nine percent chance of keeping it.

QUESTION: Was that the lesson of World War I?

VELEBIT: That is true. And it is true today: look at Berlin or wherever you want; it is a fact of history. And we, the Yugoslavs, understood this in 1944. For this reason we made our preparations to concentrate our troops for the final quick advance against the Germans in a northwestern direction, in order to be in Austria and Trieste before the British and American troops.

QUESTION: Were you in on the military planning at that time?

VELEBIT: At that period, no. I was the chief of the Yugoslav military mission in London. I was trying to convince you by diplomatic methods. I failed. It is clear, and I won't go into the exchange of telegrams and letters between Churchill and Alexander [Sir Harold Alexander, Allied commander in Italy] and Churchill and Roosevelt. That is on the record. But you must know of Churchill's passion to keep Trieste as a bridgehead in the eastern territory, because he thought that Yugoslavia was going to be allied and friendly with the Soviet Union in that period. In other words we were regarded as a satellite of the Soviet Union. That was the great discovery of the Western countries, who were as always wrong in their political assessments. But Churchill was really at the head of the crusade against the Red invasion of Europe. He wanted to prevent the Russians from using the port of Trieste, and because he identified a Yugoslav Trieste with a Russian Trieste—Russian bases, facilities, who knows what?—he was absolutely ready to fight against us—to turn his guns against us—in order to secure Trieste for the Italians.

QUESTION: Was this related to Churchill's interest in the Ljubljana Gap that he had shown earlier—the soft underbelly concept?

VELEBIT: No, I do not think so. It was related to his vision of not allowing the Russians to get a foothold in the very important European port that Trieste was. For this reason, in spite of our having fought against the Germans on the outskirts and in the town of Trieste, and our advance troops having reached the River Soča beyond Trieste, he sent New Zealanders against us, and he directed them to open fire if necessary. He did so in order to keep Trieste Italian, to keep us out.

That is a point of history which is for us, I would say, very grievous in its concept, and it hurts us even now, after so many years, that Churchill could have been ready to fight us in that period just to keep an advantage in his power struggle or strategic plans against the Soviet Union. We have some evidence, but I cannot say very strong evidence, that the British even sent German troops to hold out against us, because the Germans fought against us for two days after the armistice was signed. We feel that there is some evidence that there was an agreement between the British and the Germans on this, as it would explain the absolute stubborn fighting of the Germans at the last moment. For instance, the whole port of Rijeka (Fiume) was blown up by the Germans and sabotaged a day after the armistice. I can not prove it, but I tell you that most of the Yugoslav leaders, including Tito, do believe it is true. You have seen from Churchill's memoirs that he persuaded the American President—it was Truman by then—to back him up in this policy and to help in case it was necessary to fight against us.

QUESTION: The Americans did not need a great deal of persuasion on this because it was in line with what had been the Roosevelt and Hull policy of saving the territorial problems for the peace table, so to speak, and if you will recall, the public statement put out at the time the New Zealand troops were sent to Trieste said that territorial settlements will not be made by armies on the march. There was a very strongly held belief in Washington that the Yugoslavs were going to stay—that they were doing precisely what you said: trying to get to Trieste first in order to stay there and have the negotiations take place on the basis of a military possession of the city. From the American point of view all postwar territorial planning studies had been done on the basis of a division of that area, with Trieste remaining in Italian hands. So there was a position which was favorable to the Italian point of view already at that time.

VELEBIT: I don't want to enter into any arguments, but I want to say that after all the Yugoslavs were also allied to the British and to the Americans in the war, and if we had taken over enemy territories, we would have had active occupation forces as they did. But of course they showed us from the very beginning their, I would say, enmity or hostility: not only did they push us out of Trieste, but also they did not allow our troops to take part in the occupation of Austria. We also entered the south of Austria, and we thought that it would be equitable compensation for our efforts in the war, for the 1,700,000 dead we suffered—more than any other nation except the Russians—to have at least a symbol of our participation in the war, a little bit of enemy territory as an allied occupying power. The British and Americans did not do that. They wanted to show that we did not count; that we were just a little peripheral country. Of course that created a bad feeling. They were offending us all the time. We were conscious that we gave a contribution in blood which was terrible, yet we were not allowed to belong to the group of victors. That really hurt.

But to come back to your original question, I was in the Yugoslav military delegation. We had the first contact with the British in the little village of Duino (Devin). The head of the Yugoslav delegation was our chief of staff, General [Arso] Jovanović, and I was his deputy in these negotiations. During these negotiations Edvard Kardelj [Tito's principal lieutenant and colleague in the National Liberation Movement, and later holder of numerous high posts in the government] was sitting in Postojna, our headquarters. We reported to him every day, and he gave us our instructions for the negotiations. We were forced to accept, first of all, the *diktat* on withdrawal of the Yugoslav troops, and then we made the unfortunate—or fortunate, however you want to call it—arrangement about partition into Zone A and Zone B. At that period, I myself—but I mention also Kardelj—was convinced that we had lost Trieste, which means we were convinced that we had lost Trieste much before the 1953 date you mentioned.

The whole relationship with the British and the Americans in that period was composed of a lot of pinpricks, which accumulated from day to day and created a very tense and disagreeable atmosphere. I can tell you that with authority, because I was in the middle of that whole cold war, if you'd like to call it that, as the Undersecretary in our Ministry of Foreign Affairs. 1 was the man who set up our new Ministry of Foreign Affairs. The Minister, Mr. Šubašić [Ivan Šubašić, Minister for five months in 1945] was really a figurehead. I reported to Tito daily, and he had very little influence.

But just to make it quite clear, we were certain we had lost Trieste in 1945, but we still did not want to be pushed around. We very much resented your declaration in 1953 as well as the earlier one in 1948.

QUESTION: Had Yugoslavia ever expected the Free Territory to work, or were you waiting until a time when you could get a territorial agreement?

VELEBIT: That is a question which is almost impossible to answer, because what is Yugoslavia? Yugoslavia is a country which has a number of people in or around the government who have different ideas and different approaches. There were not a few people who believed that it might work. I can tell you, my friend Aleš Bebler, for instance, was one of those. He is a Slovene, being a man from Trieste. I am also from Trieste.

Everybody in our country has his own views, unfortunately, sometimes too many views. To answer your question about how we reacted on Trieste, Bebler for instance, who is a very intelligent man and a very accomplished diplomat, thought that the Free Territory of Trieste could somehow work. I, on the other hand, have always been against international towns. I have never seen one which functions well, and I think it is always the nucleus of a future crisis. I was always for a very realistic conception. As I said before, I understood clearly in 1945 that we had lost Trieste. For me the only realistic solution of the problem was to keep Zone B, which was, after all, occupied by our army. Without a fight you could not push us out. On the other hand, I knew that we were not strong enough to fight against the British and the Americans, plus the Italians, in order to recover Trieste. For me the situation was clear. The division was Zone A to Italy; Zone B to Yugoslavia.

QUESTION: In the fall of 1953, was it a question from the Yugoslav side whether you wanted to leave the situation as it was, with the Anglo-American possession of Zone A and the Yugoslav possession of Zone B, or whether, because of your desire to have better relations with Italy or your general position with respect to the Western countries being in more normal relations than you had been a few years before, you really wanted to get something more final—something which would be a settlement?

VELEBIT: Well, I think as far as I can recall, we would have been quite happy if the English and American occupation of Trieste had been carried on for several more years. But you, of course, had promised, in order to help the shaky Italian governments win their elections—an absolutely wrong method in my view—that the whole Free Territory would be Italian, and then in 1953 you proposed the Italian occupation of Zone A.

Now, here you diminished your zone of maneuver. You just could not break the promises you made to the Italians. For us it was useful to keep the British and American troops in the zone as long as possible, because our relations had become much better. After our break with the Russians, relations with the West suddenly became much better, and we became normal human beings again who were ready to talk to each other. I played a certain role in establishing American military aid to Yugoslavia.

QUESTION: Mr. Velebit, may I ask you two questions specifically related to 1953? First, one gets the impression that Yugoslavia's economic requirements had some role in your willingness to move toward a settlement. Do you agree? The second relates to a point which must have occurred to you, which is how long the British and Americans were going to stay there. Was it to your advantage to get a settlement before they decided to pull out and turn over possession to the Italians, no matter what? Was that in your mind or the mind of the government?

VELEBIT: Well, I can tell you only what I remember now. I think that the economic requirements did not play a role, because we Yugoslavs, you know, are irrational and we are very often ready to forgo some advantage because of some *idée fixe,* as we did in the war, when we suffered terrible casualties because we thought it was necessary to fight the Germans by all means. Here again we were as passionate, wanting to have Trieste as our main port, and righteously convinced that Trieste was a city which ought not to be Italian. I will explain how this question came into the negotiations of 1954. In the agreement which Brosio and I finally signed there is a clause about the Italian compensation. I think the Italians had to pay us about $50 million. By the peace treaty made with Italy in 1947, I think Italy was obligated to pay Yugoslavia $125 million in reparation for war damage. We foolishly permitted them to put forward a lot of counterclaims against us, and those counterclaims finally cancelled out all compensation. Yugoslavia got almost nothing but a few houses, which we nationalized, in Istria. Now I come to the point which I want to make. I proposed to my government to include in the Trieste agreement a lump sum of compensation for Yugoslav losses in the war which the Italians were to pay us, I think in the amount of $50 million.

QUESTION: It turns out to be $30 million.

VELEBIT: Koča Popović, my Foreign Minister, and Edvard Kardelj were very angry with me. They sent me a couple of telegrams saying that I should not mention any compensation in the agreement because it would be a shame to get economic advantages out of a political agreement in which we were giving up Trieste. But I am a very down-to-earth chap, and I knew that it was the only possibility to get some money out of the Italians. So I insisted on my own that we find a lump sum for the Italians to pay. Finally after a long battle which I had, not with Tommy Thompson, but with my own people back in Belgrade, who were the purists, you know, I got the permission to get this in.

QUESTION: In a confidential note which is not part of the agreement?

VELEBIT: Yes. I think that answers your question.

QUESTION: We also posed the question whether American, and to a lesser extent British, economic aid was in your mind; if there were no agreement, this might affect what you were getting?

VELEBIT: No. It was not. We hoped that the situation was going to be advantageous to us, because our relationship with the Americans and the British became better from day to day. You got more and more irritated with the various forms of Italian blackmail. So, we thought, it is quite fine for us as long as the Americans and the British stay in Trieste, for they might be ready to give us some concessions in the port. There was no economic incentive for us to have them out and the Italians in.

QUESTION: I raise this question in connection with Murphy's visit to Belgrade. The pretext of his visit was to discuss economic questions, which might have been a good way of exercising a certain pressure on Yugoslavia. Murphy delivered a letter from President Eisenhower to President Tito, which referred to "the great problems of the free world of which our countries are a part." Against the background of all the important aid the U.S. had furnished Yugoslavia and might furnish in the future—such was the implication—couldn't Yugoslavia make a minimal territorial concession in Zone B?

VELEBIT: Look, that was not the way it was. It was really a question of about a mile or so of territory. I can tell you that economic considerations of that nature did not play any role. But a very important role was played by the letter from President Eisenhower, because Tito quite obviously was pleased that a man like Eisenhower, a big hero of World War II, President of the United States, you know—if a man of such standing writes him a letter as a friend, he will respond. That is our character. If you come to us as a friend, we are ready to give you our last shirt. That is the rule of Balkan hospitality. But if you come and demand something, then we fight like hungry wolves. That is also characteristic. That letter was really very important. It changed the situation at once. I do not say that we would have not reached an agreement.

QUESTION: It was very close?

VELEBIT: A very small piece of territory, but I tell you, this gave a very nice ending to our negotiations.

QUESTION: Now, I have one more background point before we get to January 1954, and it concerns Soviet-Yugoslav relations. Stalin died in March 1953. Toward the end of 1953 and in 1954 came the first unfreezing of your relations with the Soviet Union; the beginning of events which led to the Khrushchev visit in May to June 1955. Did any of those considerations play a part in the Yugoslav approach to Trieste?

VELEBIT: Not as far as I know. I was not in Yugoslavia that year. I was sent as Ambassador to Rome in 1952, where I had a very unhappy year from a political point of view. The Italians behaved outrageously toward me. They did not want to receive me. They did not speak to me. I was not once invited by the Italian Minister or by an Italian member of government. I met only [Vittorio] Zoppi, the Secretary General of the Foreign Ministry. The only member of the Italian Parliament who had the courage to come to see me was [Feruccio] Parri. It was a shock, because I was to a certain extent a relative of the Italians. I speak Italian, being a Triestino. My cousins are Italians, professors in Padua and in Venice. I was really received with glacial reserve. It was due to the political issues, of course. My predecessor had a much happier time because he was there in the Sforza period, and Sforza [Count Carlo Sforza, then Foreign Minister] was not such a narrow-minded man as De Gasperi.

QUESTION: Well, I think we have the background, so let us discuss the London negotiations. How did you and your government look upon the possibilities of this kind of negotiation? I recall, as it is described in the study by Duroselle, there had been talk of French participation and so on, but suddenly there was a British-American initiative for a special kind of negotiation with ambassadors, wholly off the record and out of sight, with no press contacts or public knowledge of the negotiations. What was your view about this kind of negotiation? Was it something that looked more promising than the previous attempts?

VELEBIT: Yes, we thought it was more promising because we believed that the most important point of this negotiation was secrecy. The moment the press gets hold of this kind of thing, passions start to boil in all the countries. The newspapers write a lot of explosive nonsense, and it is impossible to pursue the negotiations. For this reason we were particularly attracted to the idea of negotiations kept absolutely secret. They were. And that, I think, indeed made for the success of the negotiations.

QUESTION: Who suggested they take place in London rather than somewhere else?

VELEBIT: I don't know. They offered us London and we accepted because we felt that London was quite a good place. I also think my government had a certain amount of confidence in me as a negotiator in that period. That may have played a certain role; I'm not quite certain. I don't know what Kardelj and Tito said to each other, but I had this feeling.

QUESTION: As you began your conversations, we understood from Ambassador Thompson, it was a kind of full-scale tripartite negotiation, so to speak, with advisers and assistants around the table. He mentioned that Yugoslavia presented formal demands and defended them as in international negotiations, but it was only when you decided to get down to just three people in the room that you really began to make some progress. Is this your recollection?

VELEBIT: We had to fire off the so-called *baroud d'honneur*. That was rather repulsive for me to do, but I had instructions from my government to demand the whole Free Territory of Trieste. I had to put forward all the arguments—economic, geographical, military, everything—and I rattled them off, I think, that whole first week, keeping myself busy and keeping all the others busy. I was convinced that it was just a *baroud d'honneur* to show that we were trying to present our full case, and I am quite certain that Thompson and Harrison also understood it was a method for letting off steam. We presented our case. We apparently could not succeed, but we did our best.

When they told us that the only way we could talk shop was if we came down to Zones A and B, then of course we dismissed all the advisers and experts who were sitting around the table with maps, statistics, and all that sort of thing. We met in my flat, 34 Harrington Gardens in London, in order to avoid all publicity. Thompson and Harrison came to my private residence, and there we negotiated for two months.

QUESTION: In that connection did you come with instructions which in effect said, "We recognize that the real negotiation is going to be based on acceptance by us of the Zone A-Zone B division," or did you have to go back after the opening week and request modification?

VELEBIT: Well, I had to go back. I did not go back personally but I remember very well that every day I sent long telegrams to my minister, Koča Popović. I knew very well that Kardelj was breathing down his neck. Kardelj, a Slovene, was of course trying desperately to get Trieste, or at least a part of the port of Trieste, with Bebler and Brilej [Jože Brilej, Assistant Foreign Minister], both Slovenes, backing him up. Koča Popović, a very intelligent Serb, knew, as I did, that the situation was already settled by the occupation of the territories—we had Zone B; they had Zone A—and that we were not strong enough to change it.

QUESTION: Let me ask you a question about your view of the role which Harrison and Thompson played. Essentially they were the middlemen in these negotiations. On the other hand, you were in effect negotiating with them during this period from January to May. Did you have full faith and confidence that they were playing the kind of role which would be best for Yugoslavia?

VELEBIT: I had full faith and confidence because I knew Thompson from before. I was his colleague in Rome, where he was the Minister-Counselor of the U.S. embassy, before he went to Vienna, and I had a personal liking for him. Harrison is a different type, much cooler and very efficient. I must say I became very fond of both of them and I had great respect for them. Of course I understood that they had their instructions, which were very limited, but they tried to be patient. That is very important. I caused them some difficulties, not from my own inclinations but because of the instructions I had from Belgrade. But they showed the utmost patience with me, and for this reason I had full confidence and respect in their loyalty and integrity.

QUESTION: Did your government have real problems of public opinion to cope with?

VELEBIT: Here I want to say something which may have broader importance. Governments can have problems of public opinion, but it is of course up to them to create public opinion, particularly countries like my own, where the press is controlled to a certain extent, or the Soviet Union, where it is very much controlled. In a lot of countries the big press is controlled, and the governments are able to influence public opinion to a very large extent. They can either blow up a dispute or tone it down.

I am quite certain that the majority of the Yugoslavs and the majority of the Italians—the overwhelming majority—were happy to reach an agreement for peace, because the majority of the people do not like war. After all, we had lost sufficient blood in the last war. Of course you can always find a thousand or two thousand demonstrators, for any cause, in any country, in any city. But the government can always influence public opinion if it wants to. That is my opinion.

QUESTION: The problem for Yugoslavia in this case really would not have been public opinion; it would have been different points of view within the ruling group, especially, as you said, the views of Slovene elements. Is that right?

VELEBIT: Yes. A few individuals in the ruling group sometimes play a very important role. You know, if Tito had made three or four speeches, preferably in Croatia and Slovenia, explaining the situation and the necessity of agreement and good relations with the Italians, then it would have been accepted and understood by the people.

QUESTION: I am struck by the fact that this was an almost unique negotiation in that the people who were in the middle attempting to get two parties together were not simultaneously talking with both of them. There was a long period of direct talks by the Americans and British with the Yugoslavs, and then later a separate negotiation, so to speak, which they held with the Italians on the basis of the arrangement reached in their talks with you. During the first phase of the negotiations was anybody in touch with the Italians? Did you or your government have contacts with them?

VELEBIT: No.

QUESTION: I assume from what we have heard that the Americans and British also kept the whole thing secret from the Italians. They were allies in NATO, but I understand the ground rules were that this first phase was to be kept quite separate and secret from the Italians until the time came when something could be presented to them.

VELEBIT: I can tell you that we had no contact with the Italians, as far as I know. We did not inform them about the talks. I think there was some information given to the French, but in the later stage of the talks.

I now remember what prompted us to accept these negotiations and to carry them out to a solution. It was the Anglo-American decision to withdraw their troops. When they made this decision, we understood that there was no other way than to reach an agreement.

QUESTION: When did you become aware of this? This was the question I posed earlier—whether you would have been willing to let things continue as they were if not for the announcement of the British and American intention to withdraw?

VELEBIT: I can't remember exactly, but I can tell you that when we understood that you, the Americans and the British, were a hundred percent serious in wanting to withdraw the troops at the earliest possibility, then we knew there was no more playing around; we had to find a solution. But if you had not put it so strongly, we would have preferred that you stay on.

QUESTION: The agreement, after all, was not just a status quo Zone A-Zone B agreement but involved some gains for you—a piece of territory in Zone A, along with some other advantages. Was it important for you and for your government to get that extra territory? You mentioned you wanted to get a port which would be useful to Yugoslavia, and then later I gather that the railroad was of some consideration as a means to give Slovenia access to the sea. How important was that? Was that face-saving? Was it to enable you to say that you got more than just the status quo? Or was it of real economic or psychological importance?

VELEBIT: It was of face-saving importance. The port of Žavlje, which we could not get, was really economically important for us. The few square miles of territory were of no importance whatever, except to sweeten the deal a little bit in appearance to the Slovenes and to show that the solution was not a hundred percent imposed on the basis of the actual division between Zones A and B. It was just a token of the negotiations; the difference between an imposed settlement and a negotiated settlement.

QUESTION: Let me ask you one thing on ports. The Americans and British did propose at first that three coastal towns in Zone B—Capodistria, Isola, and Pirano—go to Italy.

VELEBIT: Yes. We were ready to give them up for the port of Žavlje, because these three towns were not so important, although Koper has some economic importance and Pirano is a pretty resort. But the Italians did not want to give us Žavlje.

QUESTION: Of course, Žavlje is really a part of the city of Trieste, it is so close. It would have been something like Fiume and Sušak before the war?

VELEBIT: Yes. But the main point is that Italy wanted to deny us a good port. Here again I see the Italian policy: they wanted to have Trieste, not so much for themselves, but to prevent us from having it.

QUESTION: Another point in the London negotiations is the question of how permanent the arrangement was going to be. I gather this was important from your standpoint because you did not want the Italians to be in a position to say that things were still unsettled and maintain a claim to Zone B. Was this a difficult point in your negotiations with Harrison and Thompson? Was it as difficult between you and Belgrade?

VELEBIT: It was, to a certain extent, because there was a difference of opinion between Belgrade and me. I was at that time, and am still today, inclined to accept the Italian view—the temporary character of the solution—because I did not want to give up our claims on Trieste. Some of my colleagues in Belgrade, particularly Mr. Brilej, were advocates of a definitive solution. Although I was speaking for a definitive solution in my talks with Harrison and Thompson, I had a mental reservation because I really believed that was not the right approach. I thought, "All right, if the Italians want it to be temporary, I am for it, because why should we give up our claims on Trieste and accept this now as a final solution? Maybe in the period of our grandchildren there will be some new crisis. Why should the Italians then be able to point to the fact that we have given up Trieste for good?"

QUESTION: If you look back from the perspective of today, this agreement has worked out in the Yugoslav-Italian overall relationship to remarkably good results, wouldn't you say?

VELEBIT: Of course, because you know the Yugoslavs and the Italians both are nice people, and the North Italians, the Friulians, and the Slovenes have a similar temperament. They get along very well. Through trade and cooperative arrangements our economy has become closely linked to the Italian economy, and Trieste, which was a failure as a port, has become a very important commercial city for the surrounding Yugoslavs. I think the personal traffic across the frontier there is one of the heaviest in Europe. There are millions of people crossing every year. And in Trieste, where the Slovene language was absolutely taboo during Mussolini's time, now you think you are in a Slovene town.

QUESTION: I have one more question on your phase of the negotiations in London, and that is, was there any point during those months when there was danger of the talks breaking down? Did you feel at any time that maybe there would not be an agreement?

VELEBIT: No. I was convinced that we would have an agreement. Before I started the negotiations, I had long talks with Tito, Kardelj, and Ranković [Aleksandar Ranković, Vice President, Yugoslav Federal Executive Council, 1953–1963], the top three decision-makers. If I may say so, Kardelj was the most influential. Being a Slovene and the theoretician of the whole government, he was really the top man on this question. They told me quite clearly that we must reach an agreement. There was no way out of it. Of course in any negotiations you try to be as tough as possible to reach the maximum you can reach, and you can never be absolutely certain whether you could have gotten something more if you had insisted on it. I cannot say whether we would have been able to get something more. Of course, there were short crises during the negotiations but I was absolutely certain from the beginning to the end that we were going to reach an agreement.

QUESTION: You say you do not know whether you could have got more. Did you know from the beginning that you could never have Trieste?

VELEBIT: I knew that from 1945, as I said before.

QUESTION: When you came through the talks with Thompson and Harrison with the memorandum of agreement to be handed to the Italians, was this the end of concessions from your side?

VELEBIT: Yes.

QUESTION: You did not envisage a new negotiation in which you would have to bargain all over again, or rather the Americans and British would have to bargain all over again with the Italians and reach a middle point between their claims and the points agreed with you?

VELEBIT: It was very clear to me, as I said before, that where our troops stood we would not give away an inch of territory. On the other hand, we knew that we could not get anything from Zone A, or anything of substance. Now, the other points which were under discussion—setting up a special administration, the utilization of languages, setting up a Slovene bank and cultural center, and all this sort of thing—were all marginal. And I must say, I am still today astonished that the Italians were so stubborn about them. For instance, the Italian Fascists had burned and looted the Slovene Cultural Center, and we wanted only to have this compensated, which was, I think, a legitimate demand. The bank and educational services were also necessary, because we wanted the Slovene minority in Trieste to be able to survive.

QUESTION: Did you have any negotiating role after your talks with Harrison and Thompson were concluded in May 1954? When they were talking to Brosio, were you kept informed?

VELEBIT: I was kept informed. Brosio got instructions from his government, and he wanted some concessions. These points were communicated to me. I kept my government informed, and as far as I remember we rejected all his demands.

QUESTION: So it finally came down to just the Punta Sottile business?

VELEBIT: Yes, the Punta Sottile business. But there were a few questions about those other matters I mentioned: administration, utilization of languages, schools, school inspectors, a lot of details, and of course the question I mentioned before of the compensation of $30 million.

QUESTION: Did you feel that their demands were for concessions that went beyond what you had been willing to give in your phase of the negotiations and thus jeopardized the agreement, or that they were so small that somehow they could be ironed out?

VELEBIT: Oh, I think they were small enough. I do not think they were of any importance. I do not think we would really have lost very much if we had given them these concessions, and they would not have gained anything by getting them. Really, it was a little fight about prestige.

QUESTION: On both sides?

VELEBIT: On both sides, yes.

QUESTION: But apparently it was sticky enough so that the U.S. government sent Mr. Murphy to try to settle it with Marshal Tito.

VELEBIT: I repeat again, I don't know really how successful Murphy's mission was but knowing Tito very well, I am quite certain that Eisenhower's letter really did the trick.

QUESTION: Was agreement a foregone conclusion? Attilio Piccioni, the Italian Foreign Minister, apparently thought the thing was so bad that he resigned rather than sign. And Martino [Gaetano Martino, who succeeded Piccioni as Italian Foreign Minister] came in and signed.

VELEBIT: But it was really Scelba who made the decision.

QUESTION: Turning to a more general point, how do you evaluate the role of the Americans and the British? In one sense they were mediators, but in fact as the people who had their troops in the territory at the time, they were as much participants as you or the Italians. Is there much of the element of mediation in the talks with the Yugoslavs and Italians on Trieste?

VELEBIT: I think there was a great deal of mediation. The fact that we spoke to the British and Americans and not to the Italians, that we succeeded in speaking the language of reason and not of passion with them (which wouldn't have been possible with the Italians), and that then the Italians did not speak to us but spoke to the British and the Americans, made all the difference. For this reason—if I may say here—I would think that the only possibility of getting an Arab-Israeli arrangement would be something similar. Perhaps the British, Americans, and Russians, let us say, or somebody else such as the Yugoslavs—experts in mediation—could play the part of intelligent listeners to the grievances of one side and then take them to the other. That is the only way I see that they could reach an agreement.

QUESTION: Right after the Trieste settlement Mr. Dulles did have the idea that this was a very effective formula which might be applied to the Arab-Israeli question and certain proposals were made. But it did not work, I think partly because of the fact that the Trieste question was ripe for settlement and the other one was not. There is something in the fact that in the Trieste case not only were they mediators, but they also had a physical presence, which as you yourself said had some influence on the parties.

VELEBIT: You are quite right. It had an enormous influence. But I want only to add that what you said about ripeness is absolutely correct. The Trieste situation was ripe because both the Yugoslavs and the Italians wanted a settlement.

QUESTION: The Americans and English wanted to get out?

VELEBIT: Absolutely. That precipitated the settlement, of course. They put the knife under our throat. They said, "We are pulling out, and now you have to settle." But we were both willing to settle. We were ready to settle. And I am certain that there is no such problem, no such conflict in the world which cannot be settled if both sides are determined to find a settlement.

QUESTION: Let us look at the Trieste question in the light of Yugoslavia's relations with the West. In 1953 Yugoslavia had negotiated the Balkan entente with Greece and Turkey, which was followed by talk of some form of military cooperation with the United States. Our military aid program to Yugoslavia was still in effect. It was considered that an improvement in Yugoslav-Italian relations was not only useful but perhaps necessary for the kind of strategy which was taking shape, in which Yugoslavia was cooperating to a certain extent. In the negotiations for a Balkan alliance including Greece, Turkey, and Yugoslavia in August 1954, the idea of military cooperation with Italy was considered. Did these developments have any effect on the Trieste question? Did they tend to speed up and make the possibilities of settlement on Trieste greater?

VELEBIT: I think to a certain extent. Of course, every government pursues a policy which is selfish, trying to advance what it considers to be in its national interest. I do not say that governments usually are right in defining their national interest, and various governments have different and often conflicting definitions about their national interest. But in this case, it was evidently in the national interest of Yugoslavia to get allies against possible aggression by the Soviet Union, and I can tell you we were really frightened by the Soviet buildup on our northeastern frontiers. The Hungarians, the Rumanians, and the Bulgarians were all rattling the saber.

QUESTION: After Stalin's death this was still going on?

VELEBIT: No, but the possibility was still there, and we were rather frightened. For this reason we tried to get some form of insurance. We were not trying to get an agreement with the Greeks and the Turks because we loved them so, but because we thought that was one possible way for securing our border. And we were, of course, very interested to get American and British support also. At least the Russians should know that we were not absolutely abandoned to whomever wanted to take parts of our land or destroy us completely. This notion played an important part in the Trieste affair. It was a question whether we were going to allow Yugoslavia to disappear and become part of the Russian zone, or whether we were going to reach a settlement on a minor question like Trieste. Of course, it is much easier to give up a claim, even though painful to do so, than to jeopardize your very existence.

QUESTION: It is interesting that within a year, toward the end of 1954, when it appeared possible that Khrushchev was moving to a more conciliatory policy toward Yugoslavia, the fear of Russia began to diminish and your government began to stress its nonaligned position. Do you think if the Trieste agreement had not come when it did, it might have been more difficult?

VELEBIT: I am quite certain it would have been more difficult, because our new connection with Russia and Khrushchev's new policy made the Western countries grow rather suspicious of Yugoslavia again. I think that the moment was very well chosen. It was really the British who pushed it, you know, to the boiling point by declaring that they did not want to keep their troops there any more. But why this moment was chosen and not a year earlier or a year later, I could not say.

QUESTION: This leads to an interesting question about the role of the United Nations in the Trieste negotiations. Duroselle makes the point that both Yugoslavia for one reason and the Russians for another reason thought seriously about bringing the matter before the Security Council.

VELEBIT: That was earlier. The Russians really wanted to be nasty to us.

QUESTION: That is right. But you thought about doing it for another reason, and if it had gone before the United Nations and been debated there, could it have been settled as it was?

VELEBIT: We did not want to bring it to the United Nations. It was a threat on our part we never wanted to carry out, but just as the Italians threatened and blackmailed you on the question of ratification of the European Defense Community treaty (which was absolutely idiotic blackmail and was swallowed hook, line, and sinker by Mrs. Luce, your Ambassador and maybe by Dulles, but by nobody else), so we also tried a little bit of blackmail by bringing the Trieste matter to the Security Council. But we never wanted to do it. The really important thing to remember is that the Russians (it was Vyshinsky) said they would not accept an agreement—even an agreement between the two most interested powers, which were Italy and Yugoslavia—if it was against the terms of the peace treaty.

QUESTION: Legally he was right.

VELEBIT: Legally he was right, but politically he was not right, because he really wanted to be nasty to us.

QUESTION: We are at a point where we might look at some of the general lessons or considerations which this particular negotiation has for the general process of negotiation, as to method, techniques, and so forth. In your diplomatic career, have you had other negotiating experiences which you can compare with this one? Does the totality of your diplomatic career lead you to any conclusions with respect to the nature of negotiation on Trieste?

VELEBIT: No, I do not think I have had anything similar in my career. Never in the postwar history of Yugoslavia did we have anything similar. But I think that the whole method which was developed on the Trieste question is an interesting one which could be used, with some adaptation, in other circumstances and situations. As I said before, I think that maybe it could be utilized and would work in the Arab-Israeli dispute.

QUESTION: Because of the peculiar circumstance again of people who cannot talk to each other?

VELEBIT: If two parties are so emotionally involved that they cannot talk to each other reasonably, then they must have a third party to whom they will talk, knowing that this third party is going to transmit loyally what they have to say to the other party. For instance, the third party has to listen patiently to what a disputant has to say, and then say to him, "That is, in my opinion, impossible to achieve." That is more or less what Thompson and Harrison said to us. "If you really want a settlement, and we of course recommend it very strongly, you must talk realistically, and this is what may be possible. . . ." In that way they narrowed down the differences to a very thin margin. And in time they said, "In this margin you can reach an agreement, but you must really give up everything else. If you want an agreement, just go ahead; here it is." That is in the role of a third party in negotiations.

QUESTION: Two related questions arise here. We were talking earlier about timing. The first question is: Are there any objective means of determining when the time is ripe to move? Second, there is the problem of disputants being so far apart that it is impossible for anybody to intervene, to mediate, or play the good-offices role.

VELEBIT: Every dispute has its own circumstances. You should not allow a situation to deteriorate beyond the point where a third party can be effective, as between India and Pakistan in 1971. Third powers interested in a negotiated settlement can, of course, take measures of their own to move the parties toward it. For instance, the United States could withhold arms from Israel.

QUESTION: You mentioned in answer to an earlier question that you had great personal confidence in Harrison and Thompson. Also it is interesting that Yugoslavia had enough confidence in the British and in the Americans to be willing to allow them to play the part they did, and that the Italians had enough confidence to let them talk to you without telling the Italians what they were talking about. This is extraordinary. Most people would have been scared to death.

VELEBIT: I do not think so, because after all this confidence did not go very far. As long as we had our troops stationed in Zone B, we knew very well that there were two possibilities. Either we would be able to reach an agreement or we would just fail to do so. In the latter case, nobody could take away what we already had.

CHAPTER FOUR

The Italian Negotiator, Manlio Brosio

In June 1972 Manlio Brosio spoke with Joseph E. Johnson in his home in Turin, Italy, about the role he played in the Trieste negotiations nearly twenty years earlier, when he was Ambassador to Great Britain. Despite the passage of time, his strong sentiments about the Trieste affair were clearly apparent.

In a thoughtful statement characteristic of the seasoned diplomat, Brosio outlines the setting for the negotiations and the readiness of both parties to find a settlement. His reflections center on the key role of mediation in the settlement and on the difficult position his country was forced to assume in the negotiations, despite Italy's status as ally to the United States and Great Britain. Having felt keenly the disadvantageous position in which he was placed by participating only in the second round, after the two powers had already made a firm agreement with Yugoslavia, he explains and strongly defends his willingness to break off negotiations over the issue of a few miles of territory. But he always kept his eye on the desired end, a settlement which both countries could accept. In dealing with his fellow diplomats and with his own government he did much to bring it about.

Brosio's career was in many ways similar to that of Vladimir Velebit. An opponent of the Fascist regime, he was a member of the Committee of National Liberation from 1943 to 1944, and Minister of War in the government which was in power from 1945 to 1946. During his diplomatic career he made the remarkable record of serving as Ambassador to the Soviet Union, the United States, Great Britain, and France. Widely respected by Western governments, he was an effective Secretary General of NATO from 1964 to 1971. Finally, not content to rest on his international laurels, he was elected to the Italian Senate in 1972, where he now sits.

QUESTION: If you would begin by talking generally about the Trieste talks of 1954 as a successful negotiation, I can ask you specific questions later.
BROSIO: I would say that Trieste is a good example of a successful mediation, even more than of a successful negotiation. Of course, the fact that there are mediators does not cancel the fact of the negotiation. There may be negotiations, with or without mediators. But in my opinion what made the success of this particular negotiation was the element of mediation and the favorable conditions which allowed this element to be effective.

Another element was, of course, the readiness of the parties to reach agreement. I would stress, because I know more of the attitude of the Italian side than of the Yugoslav side, the particular readiness of the Italian side and the great sense of responsibility of the Italian government leaders of that time. At the time, if I am not mistaken, the President of the Republic was Luigi Einaudi and the Prime Minister was Mario Scelba. The Foreign Ministers were first, Attilio Piccioni, and then, at the end, Gaetano Martino. All these men were very conscious of the opportunity for and necessity of overcoming the nationalistic tendencies in Italy, avoiding conflicts, settling peacefully these very thorny questions.

Certainly the fact that men of that type were in power at the moment was extremely imporant for reaching a conclusion.

QUESTION: In that connection it has been suggested that it would not have been possible to reach a settlement as long as De Gasperi was in office, because he was much more rigorous and set on this issue.

BROSIO: Maybe. I would not pass any such judgment on this. My statement was not intended to strike any difference between Scelba and De Gasperi. By the way, I have the highest respect for De Gasperi. He was certainly a great statesman and was deeply patriotic. He was psychologically involved by the fact that his origins were from lands which, like Trieste, were under Austrian rule before the First World War. But all the same, I doubt very much that, if faced with the problem, ultimately he would not have reached an agreement such as Scelba did. On the contrary, I am sure he would.

As I said, there were two elements which made a solution possible: first, the mediation itself and the favorable conditions in which the mediators found themselves; and second, the attitudes of the two sides. I am including the Yugoslav side, but of course, I know more about the Italian side, and I have already mentioned the men and their attitudes.

Why was the mediation the more important element? To anticipate a little, I think there are three lessons to be drawn from this episode. One is the value of the mediation. The second one has to do with the particular situation—the favorable political situation in which Yugoslavia found itself, both fundamentally and tactically. And third, there was one aspect, a detail, of the last phase of the negotiation, which is in my mind of technical interest.

The mediators were big powers—occupying powers—so they were in the ideal condition to exercise mediation. That taught me that, apart from the legal theory of mediation in international law and international practice, very seldom is a mediation exercised in such wonderfully favorable conditions. In general I have learned from my experience that mediation can be successful only when there is a degree of imposition on the sides. Mediation in private law practice, as I knew it when I was a lawyer, is an action intended to convince the two sides to agree on something, and generally the mediator is not in a position to impose anything on the two sides. But in international practice, when there is a position of equality and of pure persuasion, I think that mediation is more likely to fail. I would not like to appear too cynical or too pessimistic, but I think that probably history will bear me out on this point.

The Trieste case, in contrast, had two big powers—two occupying powers—who were in a position to command the solution, and their representatives did it with great skill and with the maximum degree of moderation and objectivity they could afford in their position. Certainly they used at a given moment the amount of moderate, sensible but very effective pressure that they could afford, because of the fact that they were exercising power in Trieste. The two sides, especially the Italian side, I would say, had the alternative either of agreeing to a compromise which by definition never appears to the side which accepts it as a good one, or of remaining in a condition of inferiority, due to the fact that their land, or what they claimed and felt to be their land, was occupied by such powers.

That is how it happened. Great Britain and the United States, at a given moment decided that there was a possibility, even a necessity, for Italy and Yugoslavia to come to an agreement. And what did they do? They started discussions with the Yugoslavs, and when they reached an agreement with Yugoslavia, they submitted it to us, trying to convince the Italian government, both directly and through myself, to accept it. I do not know with certainty, and I do not believe it was an agreement on all details, but I have good reason to believe that on some essential points, and especially as far as the territorial settlement was concerned, it was a pretty precise and firm agreement.

I suppose there must have been a document that outlined the agreement between mediators and the Yugoslav government. Of course, such an agreement was inevitably conditional upon Italian acceptance, but this does not rule out the fact that the Italian government was presented with an agreed proposal, something which inevitably limited its and my space and freedom of negotiation. Such was the initial setting of the negotiation and mediation in which we found ourselves in a position of some inferiority.

And so from there we struggled with the different problems. We started with the less sticky problems and then went to the more difficult ones. That is, we started—I am following my notes here—with the problem of the free port of Trieste. Then we tackled the questions of movement of residents and local traffic between the two countries, then the special statute for the ethnic groups (that was a third group of questions), and then the less important fourth group about the cultural centers—we called them *sedi culturali*—and cultural relations. We discussed at length each of those points, and here there was room for maneuvering and compromising.

Not everything had been agreed upon between the mediators and Yugoslavia, and after much haggling and going back and forth we achieved definite improvements on some suggestions which had been made, and we got more or less what we thought were fairly satisfactory and acceptable conditions. All the time we worked on that, we had in mind the main question, which was the frontier, and what they were going to recognize as territory under Italian administration, because the Yugoslavs had asked and got from the British and Americans a change in the demarcation line in their favor.

QUESTION: They got a little bit of Zone A?

BROSIO: Yes. That is correct. It was not very much, but it was added to the whole of Zone B, which contained several towns which were undoubtedly Italian—I mean with a clear majority of Italian people. So we were aware that when we came to that point, it would be the sore point and the sad one. The mediators were both skilled and excellent men, for whom I had the highest respect and also very good relations of friendship. They maneuvered very skillfully, as they knew how to do, and kept this question for last. All through the previous discussions we continued to say, "Now, we are agreeing, but only provisionally (on each of the four groups of questions I have mentioned) subject to satisfactory solution of the last and most important question—the territorial question—which is the decisive one."

The mediators knew that, but they also knew that they were already committed on that question and there was no change possible. We guessed that, and it made us just a bit nervous, and we were proved right. When we finished these questions in the four groups and reached, as I said, reasonable agreements for both sides, we started with the territorial one. There was trouble here because we understood that they had already made their decision. There was no give and take left, at least in their minds. It was just a matter of our swallowing the conclusion, and we resisted because we thought the maximum concession we could allow was just a division of the administration (not of sovereignty) on the lines of Zone A and B as they were, even if we had ample reasons to believe that part of Zone B was much more Italian than Yugoslav. On the contrary, we saw that by the proposed lines the Yugoslavs had already gained something more than the maximum we could concede.

At this point, I will come to the third characteristic of these negotiations, because it is connected with this situation and then I will return to the second. At that moment, after we had fought in vain on all the other lands and borders, the question of Punta Sottile remained, which was, as far as the amount of territory involved, very limited: a tiny, almost insignificant, strip of land. But from the psychological and political point of view its loss would have been an intolerable renunciation on our side and imposition by the other side, because it meant that the Yugoslavs would always be at the point where they would be looking into the Trieste port. It would have been a sign of the continuous presence of the Yugoslavs, and also an excellent observation post for viewing our traffic and activity there. That was very difficult to accept. They were already very near our port, but to have them even closer would have really been evidence of the bad result of the negotiation—something which would have been very difficult for the Italian government to sell to the Trieste citizens as well as generally to the public in Italy.

So at that moment we started discussions about it. We

discussed, of course, all the questions, including the little towns which we were going to lose. We demonstrated their Italian character, and so on. At a given moment, we on the Italian side reached the conclusion that we could not move the mediators from the conditions they had set. But we decided all the same not to withdraw and not to yield on the point of Punta Sottile.

Here is the other technical lesson, which is that at a given moment, in order to avoid a full defeat in a negotiation, you have to be prepared to break, because if you are not prepared to do that, you will always lose. At that moment we were really determined, in any case, not to yield, because that would have been too much.

There was a moment at our last session on this matter—we had already had many other discussions about it—when, after an impassioned plea which was felt deeply but also deliberately calculated and delivered, after Harrison and Thompson had very seriously warned us that there was no possibility of change and about the consequences, I answered very bluntly and coldly that whatever their warning, I would not yield on the point. And so we broke. At that moment they understood that we were serious. Mrs. Luce, the American Ambassador, took action in Rome. [Alberto] Tarchiani, our Ambassador in Washington, was instructed by the Italian government to move there. Our Secretary General at the Foreign Office, [Vittorio] Zoppi, I believe, also moved. The Foreign Minister called in the American Ambassador. There were a great many hurried contacts here and there.

QUESTION: Were these moves organized with a definite purpose?

BROSIO: Yes, certainly, in order to show that we were not prepared to yield. They were directed toward the

ITALIAN NEGOTIATOR

Americans primarily, because the last moves were made essentially with Washington. Before that, at a given moment, I had tried myself to convince the British Foreign Secretary in London, and Eden was rather impressed by my very warm and sincere expression of disappointment and resistance to the territorial proposals. He tried to do his best. He called in the Yugoslav Ambassador, Velebit, but he failed. He did not succeed in convincing the Yugoslavs. So the pressure shifted to the Americans. At that moment, the Americans understood that something ought to be done, and they arranged the Murphy mission. The Murphy mission was successful, because Tito agreed, on pressure from Murphy but not without give and take, to give up this little tongue of land near the port of Trieste, and he got a bigger but comparatively deserted piece of land, with no Italians and almost no people at all, in the interior.

That was the bargain. We were already conscious that one of the possible alternatives would be that. When we insisted on Punta Sottile we knew that we would have to pay something for it because the Yugoslavs were very tough bargainers—no less tough than the Russians, I must say. So when we were given this alternative—there was another alternative offered, although I do not remember exactly what it was—I immediately suggested to my government that it choose the solution of renouncing that piece of wild land and getting Punta Sottile. The government agreed and the matter was settled.

The lesson is, I repeat, that at a given moment if you really think you should not accept a certain proposal, you have to be firm enough to show that you are serious and that you are prepared to break. You have to do this even if you are not quite determined to break entirely. Otherwise you would not get anything. This is my third point; now back to the second. Why had the Americans, and especially the British, agreed to proceed the way they did with the mediation? Why did they not call the two parties in and start discussing the dispute alternately with both—which would have put them in a more equal condition—instead of tackling the matter at first only with one side—at least on the vital points—and then discussing it later with the other one? It is my personal impression that by this procedure Yugoslavia had a position of political superiority that did not seem fair to Italy.

We were NATO allies; we were committed. We were a defeated country; we had been occupied. We believed that being a government of sincere opponents of the Fascist regime and seriously convinced of the necessity of remaining loyal allies of the former enemies of our country, we were entitled to preferential consideration over Yugoslavia, which had at that time (and still has) a communist regime—one which was then much more ruthless than it became later. We felt that we deserved the support of the U.S. and the U.K. because of a community of ideology, of systems, and of the alliance.

At least it can be said that we did not get any advantage on that score—far from it. Understandably, there was the background of the history of the war, which was still very much alive, in support of the other side. There was, especially on the British side, a great amount of solidarity among certain leaders and responsible people with the Yugoslav regime. They had fought together. The British had sent a lot of officers and agents during the war to organize and to support the Yugoslav resistance. All these people, while friendly to Italy, were more intimately linked to Yugoslavia.

QUESTION: They had been comrades in arms?

BROSIO: Yes, they felt linked to these comrades in arms. So all this, adding the fact that Yugoslavia was not an ally—because sometimes you have more interest to soothe an uncertain country than to support a certain one—put them in an advantageous position. We realized this, though not at the start. I must say that I started with a more optimistic approach, and I was taught some further realities of foreign policy through this experience.

There is not the slightest degree of resentment in what I say—only an acknowledgment of an historic reality, which I can understand very well now. I understood it with a certain regret, but I accepted it as a fact of life. So these were my experiences at that moment. I do not know whether you have any other questions.

QUESTION: Yes, I have a few questions. Actually, am I not correct in thinking that after the proposal of October 8, 1953, which the Yugoslavs turned down, things were on dead center, and it was the mediators who proposed this technique of moving them ahead? Do you remember that the French were talking about a meeting of the five powers?

BROSIO: Yes, I have checked it and I think it is quite correct.

QUESTION: The French were rather resentful when the British and Americans took the position, "Look, it's we—the occupying powers—who ought to carry on the negotiations." That leads me to the next point—secrecy. You scarcely mentioned the importance of the secrecy of the negotiations, which the others have all stressed very much.

BROSIO: That's obvious. The only thing which should be stressed is not the importance, but the success of secrecy in our case. All my experiences after that with any effort to keep things secret in matters of great importance are more or less experiences of failure. It is true that my experiences in this field are especially related to NATO, where the high number of governments involved—fifteen—makes the problem of secrecy much more difficult. I remember reading in Cardinal de Retz's *Memoirs* that the cardinal [Jean de Retz, 17th century French cardinal] himself was impressed by the possibility, which he had experienced, of keeping important matters secret, even in a comparatively large group of qualified people. I think he put that figure up to ten. That does not mean ten nations but ten persons, who know each other and are involved in the same business and the same risks. When it comes to countries, it is very different. It is almost a miracle to keep a matter secret with four countries involved, as we were at that moment, which means many government officials and many possibilities for leaks to the press. But we succeeded.

QUESTION: The fact that it took place in London was a great help? You were already there, and Velebit was already there.

BROSIO: Yes, and the fact that Thompson succeeded in coming from Vienna under different pretenses.

QUESTION: He said he told people he was buying clothes.

BROSIO: The fact is that we were all determined to succeed and knew that we could succeed only if we kept our talks strictly confidential.

QUESTION: Talking about NATO, you might be interested in a fascinating account which Paul Nitze, who is on the U.S. delegation for strategic arms talks with the Russians, recently gave of the way in which we talked to our allies within NATO about the issues of SALT.

As you know there were no leaks and apparently very little resentment. Nitze said that all the conversations with the NATO allies took place before the President had made his final decisions. Indications were given in NATO of the ways we might go, and then the President later informed them of his final proposals, which were communicated to the Soviet Union. Certainly compared to the Non-Proliferation Treaty talks, it was really kept secret.

BROSIO: I must say that I should correct in this respect my previous statement about the failure of all efforts of that kind, especially in NATO, because you and Paul Nitze are right: keeping the secrecy of the SALT talks in NATO was also a success. It was a remarkable one, because there we were in an extended milieu of countries and in a milieu which so far had had a very poor record as far as confidentiality was concerned.

QUESTION: I think the United States learned a good deal from the failure to deal well with the Allies in the Non-Proliferation Treaty exercise. But let us return now to the point you made on the order in which the London talks on Trieste were conducted. You did not even participate, did you, in the beginning of the talks in London? They were tripartite, that is U.S.–British–Yugoslav, at the beginning?

BROSIO: Yes. I think I started my contacts with Harrison and Thompson on the first of June. At that time they reported to us the results of their talks with the Yugoslavs, at least those results which they felt they were entitled to notify us about.

QUESTION: It had been going on for five months?

BROSIO: Yes, because the Yugoslavs were very difficult. I must add here, in order to dispel the impression that I am blaming Great Britain and United States or Harrison and Thompson for having yielded too much or too willingly to the requests of Yugoslavia, I think that honestly they did their best to contain and to reduce the requests of the Yugoslavs, which were in many respects quite far-fetched. That I must acknowledge. But still what they presented to us was very difficult to swallow, especially in the territorial field.

QUESTION: Didn't they also have the problem that Yugoslavia was an occupying country?

BROSIO: Yes, certainly. We were occupied and they were occupying.

QUESTION: Another thing that Thompson thought was an important factor in the success was that after the first few meetings with Velebit and the Yugoslavs, they agreed to dismiss their teams. He said, "We had a great big team, and the British had a great big team, and the Yugoslavs had a great big team, which meant of course Velebit had to make speeches in front of all his fellows and colleagues." So Thompson went to Harrison and said, "Let's get Velebit over here—just the three of us," and I think they did not even have an assistant or secretary. They just talked among themselves, and therefore they were able to negotiate. He said he believed that was a very important aspect.

BROSIO: I agree with that point, but I must say that I was never alone.

QUESTION: You were never alone?

BROSIO: I didn't need to make any show speeches, because my two assistants were people who were in my complete confidence, who felt like myself; whom I trusted fully. One was Livio Theodoli, the other was Fausto Bacchetti. Theodoli, an excellent diplomat, was the Minister-Counselor there and he is now an Ambassador. I did not need to put on a show for him. Bacchetti

ITALIAN NEGOTIATOR

had been my private secretary many years before, and was later, by the way, my director of cabinet in NATO for seven years. He is a remarkably gifted man. He was very competent on the Trieste problem, which he had followed and studied thoroughly even before I went as Ambassador to London, where I found him as a secretary.

So I had only these two men, and nobody else took part in the talks on the Italian side. From time to time Rome would send very qualified envoys—Ministers of the Foreign Office and so on—who were very cooperative, and brought to me the direct voice of the Foreign Minister and the Secretary General. They would have liked perhaps to come in on the talks, but politely I told them, better not. They were all excellent men, and I remained on friendly terms with all of them. They were extremely useful. But it would have been a mistake to extend the number of people in on the negotiations. I felt it was a good thing to keep it very limited. I do not remember whether Harrison and Thompson had anybody with them or not.

QUESTION: How much information did you have on the talks between Thompson and Harrison and the Yugoslavs? There were some indications that the British at least told the French something of what was going on, and that the French gave some word to the Italians. But I gather from what you said, that you had very little knowledge of the nature of the negotiations until the first of June. Is that correct?

BROSIO: I do not remember having very much information, not even from the French.

QUESTION: I have one further question on the role of France. Apparently Bidault, when he was still in office, was very anxious to play a role in these negotiations, as he had up to 1953. Then, Duroselle suggests in his account, when Mendès-France [Pierre Mendès-France, French Prime Minister and Minister of Foreign Affairs, 1954–1955], came in, he did not have any interest in this, and thus it was possible to conduct the negotiations the way they were conducted. Do you recall anything about that?

BROSIO: I do not recall anything about it. What I can say—and it is only fair for me to say it—is that Bidault was helpful to Italy in some phase of the Trieste talks. I do not remember the details, but I remember the fact. Bidault was genuinely fond of Italy. He had been educated in Italy in a Jesuit college in Piedmont. I remember that I met him for the first time—the only time I met him actually—in Moscow where he came as Foreign Minister or Premier. We talked; we dined together; we discussed matters; and we reminisced about our pasts. He was really interested and friendly toward Italy, and had a very good memory of his school days in Piedmont, and so on. Later he was helpful to Italy. From that background arises the implication that he might have been willing to intervene, not only for the sake of France's prestige, but also from genuine personal interest to help reach a solution which would be fair and at the same time not disadvantageous to Italy. Actually he was the promoter of the well-known tripartite declaration of France, the United States, and the United Kingdom of March 1948, which recognized the right of Italy to both Zones A and B. I agree that Mendès-France, given his background, his convictions, and so on, may have had other more immediate preoccupations, and I am not surprised that he might have had less interest in Trieste.

ITALIAN NEGOTIATOR

QUESTION: This was the Indochina period. Do you think that was on his mind?

BROSIO: Yes.

QUESTION: Another question I have deals with a point you have not mentioned. Duroselle in his study makes much of the fact that Italy wanted the agreement, whatever it was, to be provisional, whereas the Yugoslavs wanted it to be final. Was it finally not decided specifically whether it would be provisional or final, so that you were both able to accept it? Do you remember that?

BROSIO: There was certainly a question about that. But for us it was quite clear that the agreement was provisional, and as such we accepted it. That we realized that a provisional agreement may last a long time is another matter. I think we adopted the formula of "agreement about the administration of the territory," which appeared to be neutral about this issue. Maybe that is all right. I have now no definite memory about such formulas, but I am sure that there was such a question and probably we used a neutral wording which could allow Yugoslavia to give it a different interpretation. But we left no doubt that we considered the solution as genuinely provisional, and we could not accept any other kind of agreement.

QUESTION: Yet in fact it has become final?

BROSIO: Well, it is not final, because in a way it is still a lasting, provisional agreement—*il n'y a que le provisoire qui dure* ["it is only the provisional that endures"]. But lasting is one thing; final is another. In order to reach finality, a new agreement would be needed. There is no doubt about that. So formally this is still a provisional agreement which goes on *de facto*.

QUESTION: That is very interesting to me because I [Joseph E. Johnson] was one of the people who drafted in 1946, "The provisional rules of procedure of the U.N. Security Council," which are still in use. They have not been changed very much since then.

BROSIO: May I add that it is very delicate for the Italian government to accept the finality of this Trieste agreement without some amount of bargaining about it, or about other connected questions. I do not mean big questions or any going back on what has been settled on Zone B. But there are other points to be settled, outside Zone B, which I hope may be solved with real mutual good will and understanding, which I trust do exist on on both sides, and are the necessary foundation of a final agreement.

QUESTION: So the present settlement will just presumably go on?

BROSIO: I suppose so, and I think it is sensible. It has lasted so long. I am happy that it has been implemented in a reasonable and fair way by both sides—by the Yugoslavs as well as by Italy. It was intended to last. It was not intended as a short-term solution, but was also intended, by us, to be replaced at a given moment by a final agreement, with some corrections. That was our intent.

CHAPTER FIVE

Catalyst of the Final Agreement: Robert D. Murphy

Robert Murphy was thrust into the Trieste negotiations as the result of a chance meeting in September 1954 with Clare Boothe Luce, then ambassador to Italy. Seated next to Mrs. Luce at a Washington dinner party, he recounted his wartime meetings with Tito ten years earlier. At the time the negotiations to settle the Trieste dispute were stalled on the issue of a few miles of territory. At Mrs. Luce's suggestion, President Eisenhower dispatched Murphy to Yugoslavia with a personal letter to Marshal Tito and the mission of trying to get a Yugoslav concession that would break the impasse.

In this discussion with John C. Campbell and Joseph E. Johnson, held in his New York office in August 1972, Murphy refers again to his wartime meetings with Tito (which he had also described in his book, *Diplomat among Warriors*) and his subsequent interest in Yugoslav matters, significant background to his mission to Belgrade in 1954. He analyzes the factors responsible for getting the negotiations unstuck, as well as those that accounted for the remarkable durability of the final agreement. The assignment was not an exercise in hard bargaining; compared to some of Murphy's other diplomatic tasks throughout a long career, it was a piece of cake. Tito was by that time ready for a settlement, but the approach had to be made in the right way, and it was Murphy's skill and tact that turned the trick.

ROBERT D. MURPHY

At the time of his involvement in the Trieste dispute, Murphy was Deputy Undersecretary of State, a post he held from 1954 to 1959. Earlier in his career he had held diplomatic posts in Zurich, Munich, Seville, Paris, and Algiers. During the war he was chief political adviser to General Eisenhower and other top military commanders, first in the Mediterranean theater and then in Germany. After the war he resumed his diplomatic career, representing the United States as Ambassador to Belgium, and later to Japan. After serving in 1959 as Undersecretary of State for Political Affairs, the highest career post in the State Department, Murphy ended his government service as President Eisenhower's liaison with the incoming Kennedy administration.

Robert Murphy's distinguished career, which has included some high adventure as well as years of more mundane service, has earned him a special place in the history of American diplomacy. He had the honor of being the first to be named to the rank of Career Ambassador. On leaving the Foreign Service he entered the world of business, and is now Honorary Chairman of the Board of Corning Glass International.

QUESTION: Do you wish to begin with some general comments on the Trieste negotiations and your part in them?

MURPHY: I will be glad to add anything I can to the record. I am not quite sure what points you have in mind, so I think it would be best if we could start off with some questions.

QUESTION: Why don't you start with any remarks you may have regarding your role, if any, before you talked with Mrs. Luce at a dinner party in Washington in 1954? Were you Undersecretary of State then?

MURPHY: I was Deputy Undersecretary. I had, in that job, a certain amount to do with Yugoslavia because we had a number of controversies, and one of them related to the foreign aid program. I remember one of the first instances of my renewed contact with Yugoslav affairs: the Yugoslav Ambassador [Vladimir Popović, Ambassador to the United States, 1950–1954] came in and was inquiring about their foreign aid program. I said I was happy to tell them that we had just allocated, I think, $33 million for additional wheat and other commodities for Yugoslavia. He said, "Yes, yes. I know all about that, but what about that additional $12 million for wheat?" He did not say "thank you" or anything else, and it really got under my epidermis. I let my temperature drop and thanked him for his visit. Shortly after that he was transferred.

QUESTION: Wasn't the new man Leo Mates [Yugoslav Ambassador to the United States, 1954–1958]?

MURPHY: Yes, and he was first class. He had been a partisan fighter in the war and had driven a jeep at one point as chauffeur to Tito, I think. So he had a very close relationship with Tito. I liked him, and we had a great deal to do with him in the next few years. When the revolution broke out in Budapest in 1956, Mates was in every day—often two or three times—because the Soviet Union had sent a couple of divisions down into the southern part of Hungary very close to the Yugoslav line, and the Yugoslavs were very apprehensive about the possibility of their moving into Yugoslavia. As a result, we had daily conferences with Mates. I got some information from him which I valued very highly. Their contacts in Moscow had told Belgrade that there had been a very hot and heavy debate in Moscow about the intervention in Hungary, with the majority not wanting to do it. They really did not want to do it, but they felt that their whole security system was at stake, and they just had to intervene. At that time that was a good piece of information which I think was pretty accurate.

QUESTION: You remember the initiation of the last round of negotiations on Trieste. If you were in Washington, there must have been some discussion with the Secretary [John Foster Dulles] about how to deal with the problem. Did you get into the question with him after you came back from Tokyo in the fall of 1953? How was the decision made to start the talks in London in January 1954?

MURPHY: Well, really at that point I had nothing to do with it at all.

QUESTION: You weren't really *au courant* with these negotiations until Mrs. Luce spoke with you?

MURPHY: No. I had nothing to do with them at all really. And it came up, as I think I said in my book, at that dinner at Arthur Krock's [*New York Times* columnist] house. I sat next to Clare Luce, who got to talking about the problem, and I told her a few little anecdotes about our wartime experience with Tito. It might be useful to say something about that here.

If you remember, we had moved Allied Force headquarters from Algiers over to Caserta, and Mr. Churchill was very keen to bring Tito out from Yugoslavia and entertain him, and so on. This was in 1944. I think that negotiation went on for about two months. Tito was very suspicious, and, among other things, insisted on twelve bodyguards coming with him. My first contact with Tito was a happy one, when he came to dinner with me the night after his first meeting with General Wilson, Allied Commander-in-Chief in the Mediterranean. I had an extraordinary house—you know, they requisitioned tremendous houses—called the Villa Lauro. Lauro was a leading Fascist, who was a big shipowner in Italy and had made a lot of money. He was in jail at the time, so I had the house and Tito came to dinner. He came in a heavy woolen uniform of the type concocted by the Russians, with a high collar, gold leaf, and all the rest of it. It was July and sweltering, so when he came into the house that night, I said, "You know, we have a good arrangement in this house. We're going to have dinner here, and your bodyguards are going to be in the small dining room, if that's all right."

"Oh," he said. "That's fine." So I looked at him, and I said, "You know, it's very warm in here. When I'm at home I like to take off my coat. Do you mind?"

He said, *"Ist das erlaubt?"* (Is it allowed?) So he took off his coat, and we talked. We both speak German so I was able to talk to him directly, which was a benefit. And he stayed until half past three. It was a good start. That's when he invited me to go over to Vis, his island headquarters, and I had a very interesting day over there a week or so later. Actually I was about two hours late for lunch due to airplane trouble. Tito and his top officers and about twenty members of a Russian mission were all waiting. After lunch we went out in a boat. He said, "I want to get away from that Russian Committee." It was the first impression I had that he was on his guard. They had really taken charge of things and he did not like it. It was the first intimation I had of the relationship. Those two meetings in 1944, at Caserta and Vis, were the start of my personal relationship with Tito. It seemed to be very friendly.

QUESTION: From the point of view of what helps negotiations succeed, the accidental fact that you were sitting next to Mrs. Luce in 1954 when she wanted some help, and the fact that you had known Tito since ten years before and could be brought into the picture are of special interest. Was the department looking for an emissary at that time? Had they come to the end of the road and did not know what to do?

MURPHY: Well, there was a pause at that point, and they did not really know what the next move should be. Everybody felt both sides wanted a solution, but the emotions and I suppose the public stance of the two parties had created one of those locked situations, with threats they were going to move troops in. A lot of people were alarmed.

Thompson and Harrison had really done a beautiful job on this negotiation, I thought, but nothing was there to give it the final push. And what I think happened was a combination of circumstances. The letter from Eisenhower to Tito was, I think, the key to it, really. The fact that I brought it over and that we had had that previous contact did not do any harm. But I am persuaded that Tito wanted a solution. He did not want to go any further. He did not want to be embarrassed or suffer an indignity, but he was eager for a solution. That was apparent. I always resented Anthony Eden saying, "Oh well, of course the Americans went over and bought him out; they offered him all this wheat."

QUESTION: Did he say that in his memoirs?

MURPHY: More or less, yes. He did not use the words "buy him out" but that was the intimation anyway. I think that interpretation is totally wrong. I do not believe that Tito would have sold out, if he really had a conviction that he wanted to do something else, for a batch of wheat. He is not that kind of a guy. So I think that was wrong. We only got into the cereal thing *after* the decision had been made.

QUESTION: Well, that's very important. Your book indicates as much, but it was not absolutely clear.

MURPHY: That's right. I remember that I looked at it a couple of weeks ago when you wrote me, and I thought of that at the time. It is not so stated, but that is the fact. And then after the talks in Belgrade, Jimmy Riddleberger, our Ambassador there, and I went down to Brioni and spent the day with Tito and gave him Eisenhower's letter. We had a very cordial, pleasant day with him. He was so proud of the palazzo they had built and the Blue Island for swimming. Tito loves the good things, all right. He was suffering from rheumatism in his knees at this point and was not too well. She was fine, that new wife of his, and very helpful.

But anyway, Tito was eager for a solution—no question about it—and the fact that Eisenhower had personally written him in wonderfully friendly terms—it was a good letter—and that Jimmy and I had come down and all the rest of it, I think, added up to a big sigh of relief on his part. And the Italians wanted the settlement too. Nobody wanted to take responsibility, of course, for making concessions to get it.

QUESTION: What was the origin of the Eisenhower letter? Do you know who decided there should be such a letter, and who wrote it?

MURPHY: Well, several of us participated in that. I just do not remember all who were involved. Eisenhower himself was, and Secretary Dulles. I just do not remember, but we had several meetings.

QUESTION: Mrs. Luce was too?

MURPHY: No, I do not recall that she was. She worked on the Italian side more than the Yugoslav side. I do not believe she had anything to do with that letter.

QUESTION: Manlio Brosio made it quite clear that Punta Sottile was an absolute must for them, for various reasons, although I think Thompson said really they did not need it in any military sense. I gather that Punta Sottile was not as important from Tito's point of view. It was a small piece of land. For Italy it was a question of yielding or not yielding to a decision made without its participation.

MURPHY: Actually in the talks I had, both in Rome and in Belgrade, Punta Sottile was never even mentioned. There were references to a couple of miles of territory— a rockpile. As far as I could tell, on the Italian side, there was no blazing issue concerning that name at all.

QUESTION: Brosio was asked in 1972 how he felt about Punta Sottile in 1954. He was absolutely convinced that they were right to stick, and he said he recommended to his government that they should not yield.

MURPHY: I am sorry to hear that. To stick was not that important, frankly. If you attach to it the notion of going to war over this area, this is nonsense. You can get yourself in a high pitch of emotion about anything, I suppose.

QUESTION: Maybe this was just a good ploy for negotiations? In a way it was symbolic for the Italians to show that they got something; that they had not just accepted a *diktat* imposed by the Yugoslavs, Americans, and British.

MURPHY: Exactly. They wanted to show that there was a reasonable solution, but they needed something to show there was a negotiation. Although attaching that much importance to the entire issue—really to make it a matter of life or death, peace or war—I think that was ridiculous.

QUESTION: Well, they were not going to war anyway. It would just mean that there would be no solution. They would continue to have this problem hanging over them.

MURPHY: I don't know. They had moved a couple of divisions, and somebody might have started shooting some day. You never know.

QUESTION: Can we get back to your mission to Tito? Did you have a free hand more or less? Did you go with a set of instructions?

MURPHY: No. The President, as in most of the times I did business with him, said, "Work it out for yourself. Use your own judgment."

QUESTION: And Foster Dulles went along with that?

MURPHY: Well, he did not ask Foster, because he was there and did not object to it at all. "Get a solution," was his advice. They were very eager for one, but they did not say just how to get it. The wheat matter was a parallel problem which was not used for the achievement of this solution at all. What really annoyed me about the Yugoslavs on the matter of wheat was the tactics of one of their ministers, Svetozar Vukmanović-Tempo, with whom I talked in Belgrade. He was one of the most arrogant tough guys I have ever dealt with. They had been treating our military mission there really shamefully, excluding them from information that they were committed to give us about how they were using the weapons and equipment we gave to them at no expense at all. So then Vukmanović-Tempo started to pound the table and demand the wheat. They were short, I believe, about 1,300,000 tons. I was authorized to give them about 400,000 tons, but I did not do it.

That is another answer to the British charge that we gave them the wheat because of Trieste. At that point we did not give it to them at all. In the following year, Vukmanović-Tempo came to Washington, and our friend Harold Stassen was the guy who dealt with him, because the President said to me, "Well, now, you were right about this over there, but Harold Stassen is head of our foreign aid. He will be in charge of the talks here, and you sit with him." So I sat with him, and Vukmanović-Tempo used the same tactics on him. After he got through I wrote a little squib and said to Harold, "Now it is your turn to get tough," and he wrote back, "Let's get tough next year," and he gave him the whole damn thing without a quid pro quo. It amounted to about $260 million. But that had no relation to the negotiation on Trieste.

QUESTION: In your book you indicated you talked to Aleš Bebler [Acting Foreign Minister] about wheat while you were in Yugoslavia on your mission. Is that right?

MURPHY: Yes. In one of those conversations with Bebler or Edvard Kardelj.

QUESTION: It never came up with Tito?

MURPHY: Never. No. I was persuaded that Tito was not the kind of guy with whom you can adopt a line like that. It would have hurt rather than helped.

QUESTION: Is that why Velebit said in his interview, "If you come to us as a friend, we are ready to give you our last shirt. . . . But if you come and demand something, then we fight like hungry wolves"?

MURPHY: Yes, I think that expresses their philosophy very well. I noticed that in this experience with Tito.

QUESTION: When we asked Thompson whether anything else came into this bargain (U.S. aid, military or economic) or if something was thrown in to make Tito accept it, he seemed to think so.

MURPHY: Well, I suppose he recalled that possibility was in the background—that if it had to be used, we could—but we never had to use it. It did not come up. It came up as a subsequent item, and that is clear because Vukmanović-Tempo came to Washington to pursue it. He got satisfaction on the issue but on a totally different basis than in connection with the Trieste issue.

QUESTION: So there is no secret concerning aid?

MURPHY: None that I know, no. In fact, I was persuaded that on both sides—both Tito and Martino [Gaetano Martino, Italian minister of foreign affairs in the Scelba government], whom I saw in Rome, wanted to settle the Trieste dispute without further ado. Martino, especially, gave me every impression of being very eager, both for domestic political reasons and for the international aspect of seeking a solution, and he was most cooperative.

QUESTION: Was he following Scelba's idea?

MURPHY: I think so. He and Scelba were completely in harmony on this one.

QUESTION: We have heard from others that Scelba seemed to be much more willing and eager than his predecessor Pella.

MURPHY: Oh yes, that's right. I might say that the fellows down in the Foreign Office—I am not quoting names; I do not remember exactly who they were, but several—were also all for it and said so. [Vittorio] Zoppi, who was running the ministry, was one of them.

QUESTION: Were you conscious of the Italian pressure on the U.S. after the deadlock in London that Brosio generally referred to and others have also mentioned? Were the Italians really building a campaign to get the U.S. to intervene?

MURPHY: They were eager to have us intervene. Yes, I think that's clear—no question about it. But they did not need to put a lot of pressure on us, because we were also eager to have it settled. And it did not cause any debate on our side as to whether we should or should not do it.

QUESTION: We did not approach the British about whether we should or should not do it?

MURPHY: Oh sure. This was done in harmony with the British, but they were not particeps to it. They did not participate in this particular mission at all. It was our initiative. They went along with it.

QUESTION: You did not bring in the British Ambassador in Belgrade?

MURPHY: Not at all. We did not use the British a bit. Not that we would not have if we had felt it was necessary, but it was not necessary. My recollection of it is that there was no abrasion there; no resistance on their part. They were all for it. Harrison seemed to be entirely in harmony with it.

QUESTION: His report certainly indicates it.

MURPHY: Sure.

QUESTION: Did you go by way of London?

MURPHY: I went by way of London.

QUESTION: Did you speak to Thompson there?

MURPHY: Yes, of course. I had not had a chance to talk to him before that. We were also fortunate to have Jimmy Riddleberger as Ambassador in Belgrade. He was very right about the whole question. And I think we caught Tito at what was psychologically a happy moment.

QUESTION: Was Mrs. Luce back in Rome by the time you went there?

MURPHY: She was back in Rome when I got there, yes. I went right from Belgrade to Rome. I think I had two days in Rome. But, I was very fortunate to have a guy like Martino in the Foreign Minister's job. So the whole thing turned out well.

QUESTION: Would you say that, while we had a success, it was not essentially due to any special talents on our side? We were there and did the necessary, but both sides basically wanted a solution.

MURPHY: Yes, that's right.

QUESTION: How did the multiple choice which was given to the Italians come up? Was this a Yugoslav proposal: that the Italians can have it this way or that way and Yugoslavia would agree to either?

MURPHY: Yes. That came up in my talks with Tito.

QUESTION: You suggested one exchange and he said, "What about another?" Was that it?

MURPHY: That's right. The other proposition was in there and the alternate was all right with us, and that pleased him, I think.

QUESTION: So everybody got a little something?

MURPHY: Yes. Everybody got a little something, and nobody lost face, as far as I can see: neither on the Italian nor the Yugoslav side did anybody lose face.

QUESTION: It was a mutually achieved solution. Both sides wanted it.

MURPHY: And there was no material loss either way. I do not believe it cost anybody anything.

QUESTION: No significant number of people had to be moved?

MURPHY: Well, I think some individuals probably moved, but it was a relatively small and unimportant amount.

QUESTION: Of course, we threw in something to help

the Yugoslavs build a new port in the territory they got. There was a financial consideration there, but it was part of the Trieste deal; it was not an outside factor. There is one issue which I gather is in a sense still open. I wonder if you would care to comment on it. You used in your book, the phrase that the Italians wanted a "permanent settlement." They still want a permanent settlement, and they deny that this one is permanent. Brosio made that quite clear when he talked to me. He said, "Some day there is going to have to be a permanent settlement." Did you just leave it open by not referring to it as permanent or temporary?

MURPHY: Yes. That's right. But we have learned in Washington, haven't we, that nothing is so permanent as the temporary.

QUESTION: That's quite right, but I wonder whether you recall if that issue was discussed.

MURPHY: Well, I remember they avoided using the word "permanent," but as far as we are concerned, we would like to see sleeping dogs lie.

QUESTION: It clearly is in a sense permanent, but the Italians don't have to admit that it is permanent.

MURPHY: Exactly, and with the happy development of relations between Italy and Yugoslavia, there is no dispute. I was in Yugoslavia last year on another matter. The movement between the two countries is terrific. Somebody told me there were about 500,000 Yugoslavs a year who visit Italy.

QUESTION: I have a general question. Do you recall, at the time you went to Yugoslavia in the fall of 1954, that Soviet-Yugoslav relations were on the point of changing? Stalin was gone, and the Soviet regime or some people in the Soviet regime were thinking of a change in policy toward Yugoslavia, and the Yugoslavs were beginning to think of their alignment with the West—that is what it had almost come to be—as a little too unbalanced; that maybe they ought to balance it back the other way toward the middle. Did you get any impression from Tito about the current state of his relations with the Russians at the time that you were there?

MURPHY: Not really, but I think I did get one from Kardelj. I had a couple of talks with him and developed quite an admiration for him. (He was a sort of schoolmaster type.) It seemed to me that their dedication to the socialist state and all the rest of it was intact, but their apprehensions about the Moscow regime were just what they had been and still were two years later at the time of the Hungarian revolution. Their apprehensions, suspicions, and doubts about eventual Soviet reactions or actions were manifest in Kardelj's conversations. While I did not discuss that subject with Tito at that time, I am sure that what Kardelj said represented his feelings. Vigilance, independent strength, determination to stay independent, unwillingness to become a lackey, and so on, were quite natural to him. You'd expect that from him. And Stalin's mistakes stood out like a sore thumb. The Yugoslavs were not going to have Soviet domination. And they were far enough removed—I think they were in a different position from the Poles and the Czechs, who lie immediately under the gun. That added geographical factor is in their favor. The Russian definition of the security belt leaves Yugoslavia a little on the sidelines. It's close, but it is not directly a part of the buffer as are Bulgaria, Rumania, Hungary, Czechoslovakia, and Poland. It has no common border with the Soviet Union, and in that respect is like Albania and Greece.

QUESTION: In a way, after Stalin's death, Tito had pretty much won his battle. He still was fearful of the Russians, but nevertheless the big crisis was over.

MURPHY: Right, it was over.

QUESTION: The Soviet Union had participated in the postwar settlement which set up the Free Territory of Trieste. In fact all four powers are signatories to the peace treaty, and they, as members of the United Nations Security Council, had been engaged in the selection of a governor of the Free Territory (which actually never took place). The Soviet Union had legal rights in the matter, but Tito had at this point a chance to settle the dispute with Italy without the Russians having anything to say about it. Was Tito concerned about the Soviet reaction?

MURPHY: I am sure that must have been in his mind, although it was not expressed to me and I have no evidence that it was. But I would assume it was. Actually I was not aware of any Russian interference, subversion, or antagonism in relation to the negotiations on Trieste. They didn't peep, didn't say a word.

QUESTION: One of the interesting things about the Trieste negotiation and one that we have discussed with some of the other participants, is whether they knew what a great success it was going to turn out to be.

MURPHY: They were very doubtful, of course. I think Thompson and Harrison in London, and I suppose Brosio and Velebit, too, had doubts about it at that time.

QUESTION: Did you?

MURPHY: No, I really did not. So far as the closing phase of it was concerned, I felt that Tito's feeling of the highest respect—I don't want to use the word "reverence"—for Eisenhower was a very important factor.

CATALYST

Here was the Commander-in-Chief of the Allied Army, the victor of the war, and so on, coming to him and saying, "I fully realize that your negotiators made concessions which represent great sacrifices on your part, and I want you to understand that in urging this further small concession, I am not blind to the great contribution you already have made." What was proposed was something he wanted himself. It didn't cost him anything. I am sure that basically that was it.

CONCLUSION

What is to be Learned?

One can analyze an episode in diplomacy until doomsday without ever finding out just what factors, and in what proportions, were responsible for success or for failure. It is hardly possible to measure in any precise way how much the ultimate outcome of any negotiation is attributable to general conditions, methods of negotiation, the initiatives or influence of third parties, or the flexibility of the governments directly involved. Yet it is worth the effort to review the record, especially in those instances where the methods used were out of the ordinary, and the end result was an international agreement on a dispute which had hitherto resisted settlement.

In this case, the basic dispute over territory had been reduced to the point where the methods of diplomacy could be applied to it. By 1954 it was clear to all concerned that the city of Trieste was bound to revert to Italy, and that the hinterland was Yugoslavia's. The only argument was about Trieste's suburbs and the nearby towns on the coast of Istria, and here all the weight of political realism was against any substantial change in the Zone A-Zone B line in favor of one side or the other. The conflict had been narrowed by prior negotiations and prior events. By 1954, too, the international situation—the relations of the United States and Britain with Italy and with Yugoslavia, of Yugoslavia with Russia, of the Western powers with Russia, and above all, of Italy and Yugoslavia with each other—was such as to make possible what had not been so before.

CONCLUSION

As the principal negotiators make clear in their interviews, the time was ripe for a settlement. Nevertheless, settlement did not come easily. It had to be worked for. And had the negotiations not been carefully planned and skillfully carried out, they surely would have failed; if they had failed there was no guarantee that later attempts could have succeeded. It is, therefore, worthwhile to look at the techniques that were used in the Trieste negotiations as a means of understanding this particular case history, and possibly of throwing light on the processes of negotiation and mediation in general. Twelve main elements that contributed to the final outcome are listed and discussed briefly below.

1. *Timing.* As we have noted, toward the end of 1953 the state of relations between Italy and Yugoslavia and the general international conditions were propitious for a negotiated settlement. That atmosphere did not exist earlier, and it might not have recurred later. Neither disputant wished to resort to force. Both were ready, though they would not admit it, to give up unrealizable claims and think seriously of a territorial settlement based generally on a Zone A-Zone B split with appropriate safeguards for transit of goods, rights of ethnic minorities, and other matters. The Soviet Union was, for the time being, without influence in Belgrade and in Rome, and was regarded as a serious threat by both. The Trieste dispute—what remained of it—no longer loomed so large as in the past. Yet it had been shown, by the events of the previous October, that it could still be explosive. Those events imparted a sense of urgency to all parties to move seriously toward settlement.

2. *Third-party initiative.* The United States and the United Kingdom were well placed to take the initiative. Inclusion of France, which was not an occupying power,

would only have complicated matters, and its foreign policy, under Georges Bidault's direction, was too supportive of Italy to be well regarded by Yugoslavia. America and Britain were influential and on good terms at this stage with Italy and, despite the gaffe of October 8, 1953, with Yugoslavia. The two parties could not have begun a fruitful negotiation with each other. The initiative (which originated with Washington and was concurred in by London) could, therefore, only have come from the outside.

3. *The diplomats.* The four men chosen to carry on the negotiations were all skilled and experienced diplomats. They knew the issues in detail and were able to deal directly with each other without being encumbered with delegations of experts and assistants. They were also rather extraordinary individuals in their common devotion to the pursuit of a settlement and their sincerity and realism in relations with one another. Each helped by being more than a carrier of foreign office instructions, and by some adroit "management" of the development of his own government's positions, all in the interest of the common enterprise. Robert Murphy was also the right man for the final stage of negotiation. Most governments have able diplomats on whom they can call for special assignments, but do not always choose wisely. In this case the four governments and the cause of settlement had the good fortune to be served remarkably well.

4. *A relatively free hand for the middlemen.* Although Thompson and Harrison faithfully represented their governments, their effectiveness was due partly to their ability to keep the negotiations in their own hands, without the necessity of constant clearance with their respective principals. This was especially true of

CONCLUSION

Thompson. Harrison was operating at home and could check with his Foreign Secretary, Anthony Eden, at critical points; Eden, in fact, had a strong interest in the negotiation, and occasionally saw Velebit and Brosio himself in order to help push a point home. Thompson was hampered at first by instructions from the State Department that he found unrealistic, so loaded on the Italian side that he could not make progress with the Yugoslavs. He had to get them changed, and then to establish a relationship with Washington that left him enough flexibility on the substance and the tactics to do his job effectively. This is a familiar problem in diplomacy; this particular case merely showed that the role of the third party could best be played by a first-rate diplomat not too tightly reined by his own government.

5. *The two-party third party.* That the third-party role in this negotiation was played by two diplomats from two governments could have been a complicating and negative factor. In this case it was not, because there was no substantial difference in American and British policies, and the two diplomats worked in harmony. Thus they could exercise a strong combined influence on their Yugoslav and Italian counterparts. There were times when Thompson had doubts whether the British would remain firm enough toward Yugoslavia, but the common front held.

Thompson, who as U.S. Ambassador to Austria was in London "to buy clothes," had the more active role because he had full time for the Trieste negotiation, while Harrison, an active Assistant Undersecretary at the Foreign Office, was also occupied with his duties there. The American weight was somewhat greater, also, because the United States had more influence with Italy and with Yugoslavia than Britain did, but the negotiating procedure and practice kept the two representatives on an equal basis, and they presented a solid front to the Italians and the Yugoslavs. It was only at the end, with the Murphy mission, that the United States took the initiative to act on its own, and the British approved the move.

6. *Secrecy*. Every one of the negotiators, both at the time and looking back on the negotiations later, believed that success depended absolutely on the maintenance of secrecy. This was especially true with respect to territorial questions, on which governments find it almost impossible to retreat from positions that have become public, and therefore lack flexibility to negotiate seriously. The diplomats and their governments (and the French government, which was given some information) did maintain secrecy for the period of nine months or so of diplomatic exchanges. Using London as the place gave protective coloring to three of the four negotiators (two were ambassadors accredited there and the other a Foreign Office official), and Thompson somehow remained reasonably inconspicuous, and was always totally discreet. There were a few hints and speculations that came out of Rome or Belgrade, including one published statement by Tito himself (interview with C. L. Sulzberger, *New York Times*, May 9, 1954) and one major leak in Italy that delayed the negotiations for a matter of weeks, but nothing from London. All in all, it was something of a miracle that diplomacy ran its full course without publicity, and a feat that would be difficult to repeat in a comparable case. The principle, however, remains important for any such negotiation: procedures should be devised which enable governments that have taken extreme positions in public to compromise in private, and to be protected against the consequences of disclosure

CONCLUSION

until agreements are reached that the governments can successfully defend at home.

7. *The weight of the third party.* The two men in the middle were not merely offering good offices or mediation between two disputants. They were not arbitrators or impartial judges seeking a compromise or a solution in equity. They represented two leading powers with interests of their own, with a stake in the dispute and its outcome, with a set of complex relations with the two disputants, with a physical and legal position in the area itself, and with economic resources to help make a compromise more palatable. They did not merely plead and cajole; they negotiated with Velebit and then with Brosio, in each case having in mind the interests and the points of tolerance of the other. Their mediation contained an element of pressure and imposition, always politely veiled. They thus brought the territorial question onto a realistic basis with both sides. Either side could choose to break off (as Brosio did), but in doing so would have to calculate the costs in his country's relations with the United States and Britain.

8. *Negotiation in three stages.* From the start it was recognized that Thompson and Harrison would have to deal separately with the two sides. Yugoslavia and Italy could not have made any progress in negotiating directly or in the presence of the Americans and British. In either case, they would have been driven to take positions from which they could not retreat. A process of simultaneous running conversations by the middlemen with both sides, relaying statements from one to the other and seeking to bring them closer to agreement (a procedure that has come to be known as the "Rhodes formula" because Ralph Bunche used it successfully in bringing about the Arab-Israeli armistice agreements

at Rhodes in 1949) might have been tried, but was not. Italy would have preferred it; Yugoslavia probably would have rejected it. The choice actually made was suited to the chances for success: a full negotiation first with one side (Yugoslavia), to produce a draft agreement that would be the basis for negotiation with the other side (Italy); then the final stage would be to get Yugoslav agreement to any changes negotiated with the Italians, and to bridge any remaining differences.

This procedure gave a definite advantage to the party who negotiated first. Brosio felt a slight resentment that he and his country were being put in a position of inferiority, but he knew that he had to make the best of it if there was to be a settlement. Having had no part in the first phase, he was faced with the texts of a set of agreements with precious little to negotiate, particularly on the crucial territorial issue on which the Americans and British, having worked hard to drive the best bargain they could get from Yugoslavia, showed no flexibility. It was interesting that Velebit suggested that the Italians be confronted with terms somewhat less favorable to Italy than had actually been agreed, so as to make it possible to make a "concession" to the Italians when they objected. But Thompson and Harrison chose to play it straight.

Essentially, the Anglo-American decision to put the Yugoslavs first was a practical one, as they were convinced it would not work the other way round. It was the only way to get Yugoslavia nailed down to a solution that might stick. The decision was based on an estimate that the tie with Italy was firm enough in confidence and good will to counterbalance the inferior position in which that country was being placed. The position was, of course, never so described at the time.

CONCLUSION

9. *Italy and the breaking point.* Italy almost upset the procedure when Brosio took his stand on Punta Sottile and his government decided that it must hold firm. The incident was not peculiar to this type of negotiation; it could happen in any. But perhaps it had a special significance here, because Italy had been put in a defensive position and was clearly getting less than it expected. Brosio, in retrospect, expressed the view that by taking a stand and risking the entire settlement, Italy in fact made success possible. If Italy had done nothing but yield, he said, it would not have been negotiation but the acceptance of a *diktat*, and no such settlement could be durable in Italy. Italy had to have a face-saver in territorial form, just as Yugoslavia did. Once the Italians stood firm, the others had to make some hard choices, and an agreement resulted that Italy could accept and defend.

10. *Controlling the home front.* Both governments, in Rome and Belgrade, naturally had domestic problems in dealing with so sensitive and potentially inflammatory an issue. Either could have succumbed to the temptation to make political capital at home at the risk of success in the negotiation by taking public positions and blaming the other side. Both had done so in the past. For Tito and his colleagues it was easier to be statesmanlike. For Premier Scelba it was harder, since he had to act within a system of democratic politics and a free press. But Scelba was much more serious about a negotiated compromise than his predecessors, De Gasperi and Pella, had been—although we do not know whether either, if heading the government at the time, would have rejected the terms Scelba accepted. In any event, Scelba consciously avoided any excess of nationalism and was pleased to accept the final agreement, in contrast to his

WHAT IS TO BE LEARNED?

Foreign Minister, Attilio Piccioni, who resigned rather than sign it. Both governments exercised great restraint. It was a measure of their genuine desire to reach a settlement.

11. *The Murphy mission.* Shifting the negotiation to a higher level to attack the final sticking point of a tough negotiation is a standard diplomatic tactic. In this case it was well conceived and well executed. The negotiations were deadlocked, but on a point that had only symbolic importance. Prestige and dignity were involved, not real substance. The Italians thought they had to show that they would not be pushed around. Tito did not feel that Yugoslavia should yield any more than it already had, but he was receptive to the opportunity for an act of statesmanship. Eisenhower's personal letter and Murphy's tact persuaded him to take that opportunity. The proposition he made was no great concession, but it was just what Italy needed to close the deal.

What if Murphy had failed? It would not necessarily have meant that an agreement would never have been concluded, for other means of persuasion would have been tried. The negotiators in London were fairly confident that having come this far, with only Punta Sottile remaining, the agreement would not be lost. Yet the inevitable recrimination following a failure of the Murphy mission might have poisoned the atmosphere for a long time and revived issues far larger than Punta Sottile.

12. *Luck.* With so many opportunities for things to go wrong, the negotiators in such an enterprise as this needed more than their diplomatic skills. They also needed a bit of luck, especially in the maintenance of secrecy and in keeping clear of political and bureaucratic obstacles within their own governments, where it

CONCLUSION

often proves impossible to get decisions of which diplomats can make timely use. Good fortune did in fact smile on the enterprise, and for that reason its success may not easily be duplicated elsewhere.

Reviewing the whole complex Trieste case, one is tempted to reach the easy and safe conclusion that no general principles emerge from it. It was an episode in history with its own dimensions, its own historical depth and dynamics. The procedures of negotiation and mediation which were applied to it were suited to its peculiarities of time and circumstance. And those procedures have to be considered as a whole. We do not know whether any one or two or three of them without the others would have brought the successful result. Obviously factors such as timing and luck have applicability to any negotiation, but they cannot be defined so as to make them useful concepts for comparative study.

Such conclusions, however, would not do full justice either to the conduct of the negotiators and governments in the Trieste case or to the analysis of the negotiation given by the participants themselves in their interviews. No disputes are alike in all their salient aspects and circumstances, of course, and no techniques of diplomacy can be automatically transferred from one to another. The very delicacy of timing, pressure, and balancing of issues that makes agreement possible in one case argues against any attempt to define techniques precisely or to lay down general rules. The twelve points provide no blueprint or negotiator's manual. Yet it is surprising how many of them have relevance for other conflicts. The Cyprus question in 1967, although the circumstances were very different, involved a series of elements roughly corresponding to nearly all of them. The diplomatic success achieved there was, unfortunately, only the avoidance of war; the dispute remained, and would provoke war at a later time.

No doubt the Trieste negotiations were simplified by the fact that the people of the disputed area were represented only by the two governments. Rome spoke for the Italians, Belgrade for the Slovenes. If any of the inhabitants of Trieste and its surroundings favored a Free Territory or some other solution, they had no representatives of their own to say so. The situation is different in Cyprus, where the Greek and Turkish Cypriote communities are recognized parties to any settlement, and in Palestine, where the Palestinian Arabs have made good their right to participate, together with established governments, in negotiations for a political solution.

The one technique that struck observers at the time as potentially useful in settling other disputes was the two-stage negotiation by the third party with first one side, then the other. It seemed especially suited to disputes between states that were unable or unwilling to negotiate directly with each other. Secretary Dulles tried to apply it to the Arab-Israeli dispute. Others have suggested its usefulness for Cyprus, Kashmir, and other problems that have defied solution for many years.

The Arab-Israeli dispute, in which direct negotiations were for a long time ruled out by decision of the Arab governments, seemed especially suited for third-party mediation on the Trieste pattern, but only if the third party had some real influence with both sides. It was instructive that the efforts of Gunnar Jarring, with only a U.N. resolution behind him, could not be as effective as those of an American Secretary of State, who could speak with greater weight both in Jerusalem and in Cairo. That point was evident even from William

CONCLUSION

Rogers' unsuccessful diplomatic efforts in 1971 and 1972, and was made abundantly clear by Henry Kissinger's remarkable "shuttle diplomacy" that brought about the Israeli-Egyptian and Israeli-Syrian agreements on cease-fire and separation of forces following the war of 1973.

One further conclusion is not a matter of technique but of substance. The two parties and the two mediators knew that the alternative to an agreed settlement was the continuation of the status quo, with Italy eventually taking over Zone A from the British and Americans. They knew that neither party could be persuaded to accept a solution markedly worse, and that neither could hope to get anything much better. Thus the limits of negotiation were fairly narrow. Success was achieved, but in so far as the location of the border was concerned, it was not so very different from failure. But, of course, it promised much more in political relations, and that promise has been fulfilled.

Other important negotiations were taking place in that year, 1954; on the settlement of France's war in Indochina, and on the British evacuation of the military base at Suez, among others. Those disputes also yielded to the diplomatic process and ended in formal agreements. In both cases the time was ripe, as the French government, under Pierre Mendès-France, was ready for the first time to negotiate its way out of Indochina, and the British had decided they could leave the Suez base under certain conditions. In both cases, however—and in contrast to Trieste—the basic political conflicts of which the individual disputes were a part were not settled, in that the Americans moved into Indochina to replace the French and prolong what remained essentially a colonial war, and the larger problem of the West's relations with the new Egypt remained after the Anglo-Egyptian treaty of 1954, to erupt two years later. The Trieste affair was notable in that the negotiation did end it as an active dispute, and paved the way to a normal and very good relationship between Italy and Yugoslavia. Those two decades of good relations provide some insurance that even occasional flare-ups and exchanges of sharp words between the two governments will not revive the old conflict in its virulent and dangerous form.

The settlement, admittedly, lacked legal finality, and still does. The question of sovereignty was simply bypassed, with the result that neither Italy nor Yugoslavia has full title to the zone of the Free Territory that it has been governing as part of its national territory since 1954. Because an attempt to make a definitive settlement at the time was not practical, and probably not possible in view of Italy's sensitivities and the difficulties of amending the Italian peace treaty, the wise course was to settle for the provisional. But the question arises whether, at some time in the ensuing twenty years, the two parties (and the other signatories of the peace treaty) might have agreed to make the provisional permanent. It is difficult to say. Had they done so, they might have avoided the acerbic exchanges over their respective rights and titles and the deterioration of relations that took place in 1974. But to have raised the question at any time during those twenty years, given no change in Italy's views and the weakness of successive Italian governments, might well have produced a similar or worse deterioration at an earlier date. Speaking of the past or of the future, the key is to recognize and to seize the propitious time. If and when it appears that both parties are ready to give permanent legal sanction to the border established in 1954, they should be encouraged to do so.

These conclusions suggest the difficulty, both for governments involved in the conflict and negotiation and for those who attempt to study this subject, of considering particular disputes in isolation from the broader political context in which they exist. It is tempting, but generally erroneous, to think of disputes as deformations or interruptions of the otherwise normal course of international relations, to be settled (or not settled) by the application of this or that method of negotiation, mediation, arbitration, or judicial decision. The complex of disputes that make up the Arab-Israeli conflict, for instance, did not remain unsolved for decades for lack of ingenuity on the part of governments and scholars in devising possible methods of negotiation. As some of the underlying factors change, the skilled negotiators and the appropriate methods may be found. In the case of Trieste it appears that, together with the choice of techniques and their skillful use, it was the fact of a changing political context, recognized as favorable when it finally became so, that provided the key to success. It made the negotiation possible, and in the end made it durable.

APPENDIX A

Memorandum of Understanding between the Governments of Italy, the United Kingdom of Great Britain and Northern Ireland, the United States of America and Yugoslavia Regarding the Free Territory of Trieste.[1]

1. Owing to the fact that it has proved impossible to put into effect the provisions of the Italian Peace Treaty relating to the Free Territory of Trieste, the Governments of the United Kingdom, the United States and Yugoslavia have maintained since the end of the war military occupation and government in Zones A and B of the Territory. When the Treaty was signed, it was never intended that these responsibilities should be other than temporary and the Governments of Italy, the United Kingdom, the United States and Yugoslavia, as the countries principally concerned, have recently consulted together in order to consider how best to bring the present unsatisfactory situation to an end. As a result they have agreed upon the following practical arrangements.

2. As soon as this Memorandum of Understanding has been initialled and the boundary adjustments provided by it have been carried out, the Governments of the United Kingdom, the United States and Yugoslavia will terminate military government in Zones A and B of the Territory. The Governments of the United Kingdom and the United States

[1] United Nations, Treaty Series, vol. 235 (1956), n. 3297.

APPENDIX A

will withdraw their military forces from the area north of the new boundary and will relinquish the administration of that area to the Italian Government. The Italian and Yugoslav Governments will forthwith extend their civil administration over the area for which they will have responsibility.

3. The boundary adjustments referred to in paragraph 2 will be carried out in accordance with the map at ANNEX I.[2] A preliminary demarcation will be carried out by representatives of Allied Military Government and Yugoslav Military Government as soon as this Memorandum of Understanding has been initialled and in any event within three weeks from the date on initialling. The Italian and Yugoslav Governments will immediately appoint a Boundary Commission to effect a more precise demarcation of the boundary in accordance with the map at ANNEX I.

4. The Italian and Yugoslav Governments agree to enforce the Special Statute contained in ANNEX II.

5. The Italian Government undertakes to maintain the Free Port at Trieste in general accordance with the provisions of Articles 1–20 of ANNEX VIII of the Italian Peace Treaty.

6. The Italian and Yugoslav Governments agree that they will not undertake any legal or administrative action to prosecute or discriminate against the person or property of any resident of the areas coming under their civil administration in accordance with this Memorandum of Understanding for past political activities in connexion with the solution of the problem of the Free Territory of Trieste.

7. The Italian and Yugoslav Governments agree to enter into negotiations within a period of two months from the date of initialling of this Memorandum of Understanding with a view to concluding promptly an agreement regulat-

[2] Not reproduced here.

APPENDIX A

ing local border traffic, including facilities for the movement of the residents of border areas by land and by sea over the boundary for normal commercial and other activities and for transport and communications. This agreement shall cover Trieste and the area bordering it. Pending the conclusion of such agreement, the competent authorities will take, each within their respective competence, appropriate measures in order to facilitate local border traffic.

8. For a period of one year from the date of initialling of this Memorandum of Understanding persons formerly resident (*pertinenti-zavičajni*) in the areas coming under the civil administration either of Italy or of Yugoslavia shall be free to return immediately thereto. Any persons so returning, as also any such who have already returned, shall enjoy the same rights as the other residents of these areas. Their properties and assets shall be at their disposal, in accordance with existing law, unless disposed of by them in the meantime. For a period of two years from the date of initialling of this Memorandum of Understanding, persons formerly resident in either of these areas and who do not intend returning thereto, and persons presently resident in either area who decide within one year from the date of initialling of this Memorandum of Understanding to give up such residence, shall be permitted to remove their movable property and transfer their funds. No export or import duties or any other tax will be imposed in connexion with the moving of such property. Persons wherever resident who decide to sell their movable and immovable property within two years from the date of initialling of this Memorandum of Understanding will have the sums realised from the sale of such property deposited in special accounts with the National Banks of Italy or Yugoslavia. Any balance between these two accounts will be liquidated by the two Governments at the end of the two year period. Without prejudice to the immediate implementation of the provisions of this para-

APPENDIX A

graph the Italian and Yugoslav Governments undertake to conclude a detailed agreement within six months of the date of initialling of this Memorandum of Understanding.

9. This Memorandum of Understanding will be communicated to the Security Council of the United Nations.

London, the 5th of October, 1954

L. E. T.
(LLEWELLYN E. THOMPSON)
M. B.
(MANLIO BROSIO)
G. W. H.
(GEOFFREY W. HARRISON)
V. V.
(DR. VLADIMIR VELEBIT)

ANNEX II
Special Statute

Whereas it is the common intention of the Italian and Yugoslav Governments to ensure human rights and fundamental freedoms without discrimination of race, sex, language and religion in the areas coming under their administration under the terms of the present Memorandum of Understanding, it is agreed:

1. In the administration of their respective areas the Italian and Yugoslav authorities shall act in accordance with the principles of the Universal Declaration of Human Rights adopted by the General Assembly of the United Nations on the 10th of December, 1948, so that all inhabitants of the two areas without discrimination may fully enjoy the fundamental rights and freedoms laid down in the aforesaid Declaration.

APPENDIX A

2. The members of the Yugoslav ethnic group in the area administered by Italy and the members of the Italian ethnic group in the area administered by Yugoslavia shall enjoy equality of rights and treatment with the other inhabitants of the two areas.

This equality implies that they shall enjoy:
(a) equality with other citizens regarding political and civil rights as well as other human rights and fundamental freedoms guaranteed by Article 1;
(b) equal rights in acquiring or performing any public services, functions, professions and honours;
(c) equality of access to public and administrative office; in this regard the Italian and Yugoslav administrations will be guided by the principle of facilitating for the Yugoslav ethnic group and for the Italian ethnic group, respectively, under their administration a fair representation in administrative positions, and especially in those fields, such as the inspectorate of schools, where the interests of such inhabitants are particularly involved;
(d) equality of treatment in following their trade or profession in agriculture, commerce, industry or any other field, and in organising and operating economic associations and organisations for this purpose. Such equality of treatment shall concern also taxation. In this regard persons now engaged in a trade or profession who do not possess the requisite diploma or certificate for carrying on such activities, shall have four years from the date of initialling of the present Memorandum of Understanding within which to acquire the necessary diploma or certificate. They will not be prevented from exercising their trade or profession because of failure to have the requisite documents unless they have failed to acquire them within the aforementioned four year period;

APPENDIX A

(e) equality of treatment in the use of languages as defined in Article 5 below;

(f) equality with other citizens in the general field of social assistance and pensions (sickness benefits, old age and disability pensions including disabilities resulting from war, and pensions to the dependents of those killed in war).

3. Incitement to national and racial hatred in the two areas is forbidden and any such act shall be punished.

4. The ethnic character and the unhampered cultural development of the Yugoslav ethnic group in the Italian administered area and of the Italian ethnic group in the Yugoslav administered area shall be safeguarded.

(a) They shall enjoy the right to their own press in their mother tongue;

(b) the educational, cultural, social and sports organisations of both groups shall be free to function in accordance with the existing laws. Such organisations shall be granted the same treatment as those accorded to other corresponding organisations in their respective areas, especially as regards the use of public buildings and radio and assistance from public financial means; and the Italian and Yugoslav authorities will endeavour to ensure to such organisations the continued use of the facilities they now enjoy, or of comparable facilities;

(c) kindergarten, primary, secondary and professional school teaching in the mother tongue shall be accorded to both groups. Such schools shall be maintained in all localities in the Italian administered area where there are children members of the Yugoslav ethnic group, and in all localities in the Yugoslav administered area where there are children members of the Italian ethnic group. The Italian and Yugoslav Governments agree to maintain the existing schools as set out in the list attached hereto[3] for the ethnic groups in the area under their

---

[3] Not reproduced here.

APPENDIX A

administration and will consult in the Mixed Committee provided for in the final Article of this Statute before closing any of these schools.

Such schools shall enjoy equality of treatment with other schools of the same type in the area administered, respectively, by Italy and Yugoslavia as regards provision of textbooks, buildings and other material means, the number and position of teachers and the recognition of diplomas. The Italian and Yugoslav authorities shall endeavour to ensure that the teaching in such schools will be performed by teachers of the same mother tongue as the pupils.

The Italian and Yugoslav authorities will promptly introduce whatever legal prescriptions may be necessary so that the permanent organisation of such schools will be regulated in accordance with the foregoing provisions. Italian speaking teachers, who on the date of the initialling of the present Memorandum of Understanding are employed as teachers in the educational system of the Yugoslav administered area and Slovene speaking teachers who on the said date are employed as teachers in the educational system of the Italian administered area shall not be dismissed from their positions for the reason that they do not possess the requisite teaching diploma. This extraordinary provision shall not be used as a precedent or be claimed to apply to any cases other than the categories specified above. Within the framework of their existing laws the Yugoslav and Italian authorities will take all reasonable measures to give the aforementioned teachers an opportunity, as provided in Article 2 (*d*) above, to qualify for the same status as regular members of the teaching staff.

The educational programmes of such schools must not be directed at interfering with the national character of the pupils.

5. Members of the Yugoslav ethnic group in the area administered by Italy and members of the Italian ethnic group

APPENDIX A

in the area administered by Yugoslavia shall be free to use their language in their personal and official relations with the administrative and judicial authorities of the two areas. They shall have the right to receive from the authorities a reply in the same language; in verbal replies, either directly or through an interpreter; in correspondence, a translation of the replies at least is to be provided by the authorities.

Public documents concerning members of these ethnic groups, including court sentences, shall be accompanied by a translation in the appropriàte language. The same shall apply to official announcements, public proclamations and publications.

In the area under Italian administration inscriptions on public institutions and the names of localities and streets shall be in the language of the Yugoslav ethnic group as well as in the language of the administering authority in those electoral districts of the Commune of Trieste and in those other communes where the members of that ethnic group constitute a significant element (at least one quarter) of the population; in those communes in the area under Yugoslav administration where the members of the Italian ethnic group are a significant element (at least one quarter) of the population such inscriptions and names shall be in Italian as well as in the language of the administering authority.

6. The economic development of the Yugoslav ethnic population in the Italian administered area and of the Italian ethnic population in the Yugoslav administered area shall be secured without discrimination and with a fair distribution of the available financial means.

7. No change should be made in the boundaries of the basic administrative units in the areas which come under the civilian administration of Italy or Yugoslavia with a view to prejudicing the ethnic composition of the units concerned.

8. A special Mixed Yugoslav-Italian Committee shall be established for the purpose of assistance and consultation

APPENDIX A

concerning problems relating to the protection of the Yugoslav ethnic group in the area under Italian administration and of the Italian ethnic group in the area under Yugoslav administration. The Committee shall also examine complaints and questions raised by individuals belonging to the respective ethnic groups concerning the implementation of this Statute.

The Yugoslav and Italian Governments shall facilitate visits by the Committee to the area under their administration and grant it every facility for carrying out its responsibilities.

Both Governments undertake to negotiate forthwith detailed regulations governing the functioning of the Committee.

London, the 5th of October, 1954

M. BROSIO
VLADIMIR VELEBIT

APPENDIX B

Letter from President Eisenhower to Marshal Tito, delivered in Belgrade, Yugoslavia, by Ambassador Robert D. Murphy, September 1954.[1]

Denver, Colorado
September 10, 1954

Dear Mr. President:

I have asked my friend and your friend, Robert Murphy, to go to Belgrade to discuss with you the Trieste settlement which has been under negotiation during the past seven or eight months, and to ask your assistance in bringing these delicate negotiations to a successful conclusion now. The British and ourselves have been occupying the perhaps unenviable position of intermediaries in this sensitive negotiation. Throughout, we have been most frank in the Trieste negotiations which we regarded as a grave responsibility to be worked out to the mutual advantage of Yugoslavia and Italy.

In stressing the importance to Europe and to the United States of a prompt and happy termination of the long, drawn-out negotiation regarding Trieste, I count on your continued wisdom and statesmanship. You understand, I am sure, better than I can describe, the larger issues weighing on the free world of which our countries are part. As you know, the United States is providing massive support in Europe to promote collective security which benefits both our countries. The American aid program for your country is not inconsiderable. It is because of our close association and cooperation in the economic and military fields that I feel it is appropriate to call on you in this friendly fashion to intervene personally in the Trieste negotiations to settle

[1] Copy provided by courtesy of Eisenhower Library, Abilene, Kansas.

APPENDIX B

the exceedingly small differences now remaining. These are overshadowed by the larger considerations affecting us all.

I believe that if you can see your way clear to allowing the Italians the small bit of coastline on the Adriatic, together with some hinterland from the strip of Zone A which they were to have given up under the May 31 proposal, we could achieve a settlement which would work to the great advantage of both Yugoslavia and Italy and strengthen your position in that area. Under the proposal I have in mind, the Italians would forego the segments of the Yugoslav Zone which they were to have received. Thus Yugoslavia would give up none of Zone B and would receive a strip of Zone A in the Muggia Peninsula, just inland from the coast.

I fully realize that in the London negotiation from February 2 to May 31, your negotiators made concessions which represent great sacrifices on your part, and I want you to understand that in urging this further small concession I am not blind to the great contribution you have already made. In my judgment, however, a settlement is not otherwise obtainable. The result, I feel sure, would redound to the advantage of your country. As a military man, you will understand that if the Trieste problem is settled, it will be possible to create a greater power toward defense in that area than if the Trieste question is not settled; and American assistance can therefore be spent with maximum effectiveness only if a settlement is achieved.

I have been told of certain economic developments and emergencies which have been brought to the attention of our people. I have asked Mr. Murphy to review these matters with you in a spirit of sympathy.

With my warm personal greetings and best wishes,

Sincerely,
Dwight D. Eisenhower

His Excellency
Marshal Josip Broz-Tito
President of the Federal People's
Republic of Yugoslavia
Belgrade

APPENDIX C

Letter of Instructions from Acting Secretary of State W. B. Smith to Ambassador Thompson, January 28, 1954.[1]

My dear Mr. Ambassador:

As United States representative at the United States-United Kingdom-Yugoslav discussions on Trieste in London, your mission is to work out if possible a permanent settlement of the Trieste problem that will be acceptable to both Yugoslavia and Italy, and that will contain the minimum seeds of future controversy.

You should be guided by the following principles in conducting the negotiations:

1. We want to put the Trieste problem in the larger context of an over-all Italo-Yugoslav rapprochement which, ideally, would lead ultimately to Italian membership of, or association with the Turkish-Greek-Yugoslav defense pact.

While it is not the purpose of this paper to suggest negotiating tactics, we believe that the United States-United Kingdom should make clear at the outset that they are not thinking in terms of a local settlement, or even of Italo-Yugoslav relations alone, but rather of the political, military, and economic health of a key area which will have great significance for all of the free world and for the worldwide effort to throw back Soviet expansion. The implica-

[1] NA 750G. 00/1-2854.

APPENDIX C

tions of a failure to find a mutual accommodation between powers which are or should be destined by geography and strategy to be close partners if Soviet expansionism is to be successfully resisted in their parts of the world, are of a very serious character. On the other hand, the benefits of a successful settlement would be very great. There is no form of pressure against the Soviet system so powerful or so effective as the demonstration of unity among countries of the free world, and there is no part of the free world, except for the relations between France and Germany, where that demonstration would have more profound significance in the eyes of the Kremlin than in the area of Yugoslavia and Italy. And there is nothing so infectious as the force of example. We are therefore seeking a "package deal" which would put Italo-Yugoslav relations on a permanently sound basis. We believe also that a package deal will enable both parties to accept sacrifices in a Trieste settlement that neither could accept if the deal were narrowly confined to the Trieste problem.

The United States-United Kingdom should also make clear at the outset that when they made their October 8, 1953 declaration they had reason to assume that it would be acceptable to the Yugoslavs. If it seems desirable, they may wish to point out that Tito in his September 22, 1952 interview with Eden actually said that he could accept a division along the lines of the present zonal boundaries. Admittedly the United States-United Kingdom did make an error of judgment, but the fact remains that the present situation is in large measure the responsibility of all three of the occupying powers, as it is certainly in the interest of all three of them that a permanently acceptable solution be reached. However, the United States-United Kingdom have refrained from putting the October 8 declaration into effect, on the principle that the best solutions are agreed ones. At some point during the discussion it may become necessary, perhaps through different channels, to make known to the

APPENDIX C

Yugoslavs that they can hardly expect to reject an agreed solution without putting the United States-United Kingdom in a position where they would have no recourse but to go back to the October 8 declaration. The United States-United Kingdom cannot be expected to withdraw the October 8 declaration, except on the basis of a generally acceptable alternative.

A package settlement might include:

(a) Reciprocal guarantees of minority rights.

(b) A broad trade agreement which would substantially increase Italo-Yugoslav trade, with suitable clearing arrangements. There should also be economic arrangements which would encourage Yugoslav purchases of the products of Trieste industry and the maximum Yugoslav use of Trieste facilities, in addition to any area of the port where they may have special rights. A fishing agreement might be included.

(c) Military cooperation, including if possible early staff talks.

By a "package deal" we do not of course mean a single document or one agreement, but rather a series of agreements.

2. We want so far as possible to draw an ethnic line which will give the Italians a continuous coastal strip including Capodistria, Isola, and Pirano, but which would so far as possible avoid giving detached enclaves to either in the territory of the other (suitable guarantees of minority rights must take care of such groups).

3. The Yugoslavs should have a suitable area in the port for their exclusive use with secure access to it by a rail link over which they would have an assured right-of-way and right-of-maintenance. We would not exclude the cession of a port area and a "corridor" to the Yugoslavs if it seems essential to the success of the negotiations, but would hope that the exclusive use of a suitable area, together with a rail link, could be arranged on a lease basis (say, for 99 years).

APPENDIX C

The port area should be sufficiently advantageous to encourage Yugoslav use of it, with facilities for economic turnaround of ships, and suitable warehouse, processing, and switching space. The possibility of United States assistance out of Trieste counterpart funds, if necessary to create a suitable area with adequate rail access, should be considered.

4. If a basic tripartite understanding for the settlement of the Trieste problem were reached, the so-called Pella proposal would then be brought into operation, by asking for an Italian representative to come to London, or elsewhere if circumstances should make a change of venue desirable. He would not, of course, be presented with a *fait accompli*, but it is believed that the Italians have given sufficient indication that they could accept a settlement along the lines described in this paper to justify the three occupying powers in agreeing *ad referendum* on the essentials of a settlement before the Italians are brought in. The final agreement might be applied by the three powers, as occupying powers, redefining the Zone boundaries, the Yugoslavs might then annex the newly defined Zone B, and Zone A might concurrently be turned over to the Italians on the assumption that after holding it for a token period they might annex it.

5. The United States-United Kingdom should hold to the position that the Yugoslavs cannot claim the right to do as they want in Zone B without conceding the United States-United Kingdom right to dispose of Zone A as they deem appropriate. With that understanding, we should indicate that we are prepared to discuss with them any proposals they may wish to make.

6. The United States-United Kingdom should discourage any Yugoslav proposal for "autonomy" for Zones A or B or any parts of them, as creating a situation without sufficient assurance of stability to be in the interest of either Yugo-

APPENDIX C

slavia or Italy. You should endeavor to persuade the Yugoslavs that their preoccupations concerning the Slovene minority in Italian territory can best be satisfied by a firm and explicit agreement on minorities.

Sincerely,
W. B. Smith
Acting Secretary

The Honorable
Llewellyn E. Thompson, Jr.
American Ambassador,
American Embassy,
Vienna

APPENDIX D

Announcement of Agreement, Department of State Press Release 554, dated October 5, 1954

At noon today in London a Memorandum of Understanding on Trieste was initialed by representatives of the Governments of the United States, the United Kingdom, Italy and Yugoslavia. Llewellyn E. Thompson, United States Ambassador to Austria, initialed the Memorandum of Understanding for the United States and Mr. Geoffrey Harrison, Assistant Under Secretary of State in the British Foreign Office, initialed for the United Kingdom. The Ambassadors of Italy and Yugoslavia in London, Signor Manlio Brosio and Dr. Vladimir Velebit, initialed the document for their two Governments. The text of the Memorandum of Understanding is being communicated to the Security Council of the United Nations.

Today's initialing came as a successful conclusion to conversations among the four Governments which have been carried on for eight months in an endeavor to work out arrangements for the Free Territory of Trieste which would be acceptable to the Governments of Italy and Yugoslavia. The United States Government welcomes the understanding reached today which it believes will lead to improved relations and closer cooperation between Italy and Yugoslavia. The United States Government takes this opportunity to declare it will give no support to claims of either Yugoslavia or Italy to territory under the sovereignty or administration of the other. The United States Government is confident that it will be possible for the two countries to

APPENDIX D

resolve any outstanding problems by friendly negotiations in a spirit of mutual understanding.

Arrangements are being made for the early termination of Allied Military Government, the withdrawal of American and British forces from the area under their occupation and the assumption by Italy and Yugoslavia of responsibility in the areas as defined by the agreement initialed today.

INDEX

aid. *See* United States, aid to Yugoslavia
Alexander, Sir Harold, 84
Allies: relations with Italy, 6–7, 10; relations with Yugoslavia, 7, 10–12, 84–88, 119–20
Alto Adige dispute, 41–42
Arab-Israeli dispute, 39–41, 43, 74–75, 104, 108, 150–51

Bacchetti, Fausto, 123–24
Balkan alliance, 12, 60, 66, 105–106
Bandung conference, 42
bargaining, 16–19, 27–31, 35, 63, 91–92, 98–99, 101–103, 115–18, 140–41
bargaining strategies. *See* negotiating strategies
Bebler, Aleš, 88, 95, 137
Bidault, Georges, 48, 124–25, 147
Brilej, Jože, 95, 100
Brosio, Manlio, 17, 29, 54, 57, 61, 64, 65, 74, 110–27; diplomatic career of, 111; negotiating instructions to, 102
Bunche, Ralph, 150–51

Campbell, John C., 23, 45, 76, 128
Capodistria. *See* Koper
Christian Democratic Party, Italian, 39, 67–68
Churchill, Winston, 7, 84–86, 131
Climate of the Trieste negotiations, 11–13
cold war, effect on Trieste dispute of, 9–12, 84–86
concessions in the Trieste negotiations, 26–31, 61–62, 63, 91–92, 98–99, 101–102, 115–16, 118
Council of Foreign Ministers, 7, 13

Cyprus dispute, 74–75, 154–55

Dalton, Hugh, 72
de Gasperi, Alcide, 57, 61, 68, 93, 112, 152
Delegations, size of, 26–27, 49–50, 94–95, 123–24
de Retz, Jean, 121
Devin. *See* Duino
diktat, 28, 34–35, 65, 87, 135, 152
diplomacy: secrecy in, 121–22; timing as a factor in, 73
disputes, formula for settlement of, 39–40, 43, 74–75, 104, 108, 155–56. *See also* Alto Adige dispute; Arab-Israeli dispute; Cyprus dispute; Kashmir dispute; Trieste dispute
domestic politics, effect on Trieste negotiations of, 13, 37–39, 51, 57, 67–68, 149, 152–53
Duino, 87
Dulles, John Foster, 18, 35, 46, 74–75, 131; role in Trieste negotiations, 24, 43, 134, 136; views on Trieste settlement, 39–40, 43
Duroselle, J. B., 38, 58, 83, 93, 107, 125, 126

Eden, Anthony, 11, 45, 46, 72, 74, 75, 133; role in Trieste negotiations, 54, 64, 69, 118, 148
Einaudi, Luigi, 111
Eisenhower, Dwight D.: letter to Tito, 18–19, 64–65, 92, 133–34, 143–44, 153; "Open Skies" proposal, 44; text of letter to Tito, 168–69
European Defense Community, 18, 56, 66, 67, 107

INDEX

Fiume, 5, 85, 99
France, role in Trieste negotiations of, 47, 48, 57–58, 98, 120, 124–25, 146–47
Free Territory of Trieste, 9–12, 50, 87–89; creation of, 8–9, 82, 88–89; zones of, 10–11

Great Britain: instructions to Harrison, 47–48, 55; relations with U.S., 43–46, 55–56; third-party role, 40–41, 49, 103–104, 113–14, 119–20
Greece, entente with Yugoslavia and Turkey, 12, 60, 66, 106

Harrison, Sir Geoffrey, W., 14, 17, 33, 43, 45–75, 95–96, 108, 117, 139, 147–49; diplomatic career, 46; freedom to negotiate, 54–55, 147–48; instructions to, 47–48, 55; relations with Thompson, 43, 46, 54–55
Hull, Cordell, 86

initiatives for the Trieste negotiations, 13–14, 25, 46–48
instructions: to Brosio, 102; to Harrison, 47–48, 55; to Murphy, 136; to Thompson, 14–15, 26, 33–34, 147–48, 170–74; to Velebit, 36, 94–95, 96
intermediaries. See third parties
International politics, as context of Trieste negotiations, 45, 60–61, 66–68, 75, 92–93, 105–107, 119–20, 141–42, 145–46
Isola. See Izola
Isonzo River, 5, 78, 81, 85
issues of the Trieste negotiations, 37–38, 50–51, 102, 114–17
Istria, 4, 81
Italy: Christian Democratic Party, 39, 67–68; demands in the Trieste negotiations, 18, 29–31, 34–35, 37–38, 61; factors in willingness to negotiate on Trieste, 13, 38–39, 52–53, 71–72, 104–105, 111–12, 138, 156; negotiation with U.S. and Great Britain on Trieste, 17–20, 28–31, 61–63, 114–19
Izola, 16, 27, 99

Johnson, Joseph E., 23, 31, 76, 110, 126, 128
Jovanović, Arso, 87
Julian March region, 4–5, 77–80; ethnic composition of, 5, 81

Kardelj, Edvard, 87, 91, 94, 95, 101, 137, 142
Kashmir dispute, 155
Khrushchev, Nikita, 36, 106–107
Kirkpatrick, Sir Ivone, 55
Koper, 16, 27, 59, 99
Krock, Arthur, 131

Lagosta. See Lastovo
Lastovo, 81
Lazaret. See Lazzaretto
Lazzaretto, 19, 63
leaks, 32–33, 56, 121–22, 149. See also secrecy
Lebel, Claude, 58
Ljubljana Gap, 12, 85
London, as site for the Trieste negotiations, 33, 47, 94
Luce, Clare Boothe, 24, 25, 37, 107, 117, 128, 131, 134, 139–40
luck, role in negotiations, 153–54

Malenkov, Georgi, 60
Martino, Gaetano, 103, 111, 117, 138, 140
Mates, Leo, 130–31
mediation: conditions necessary for success of, 112–14; in the Trieste negotiations, 47–49, 63–64, 69–70, 95–98, 103–104, 108–109, 111–14, 150. See also third parties
mediators, influence of, 104, 113–14, 150. See also third parties
Mendès-France, Pierre, 125, 156
method. See procedure
Middle East conflict. See Arab-Israeli dispute
Milje. See Muggia

178

INDEX

Mosely, Philip E., 26
Muggia, 16, 62
Murphy, Robert D., 128–44; *Diplomat among Warriors*, 128; diplomatic career of, 129; mission to Tito, 18–19, 24, 28–29, 31, 64, 70, 118; wartime meeting with Tito, 131–32, 134
Mussolini, 6

nationalism, 5
negotiating strategies, 14–16, 26–30, 54–55, 61–62, 67, 101, 118–19. *See also* bargaining
negotiations: breakdowns in, 117–19, 152; luck as a factor in, 153–54; procedures for, 39–41, 150–51, 155–56; role of the press in, 56, 93–94, 121; secrecy of, 25, 29, 32–33; strategies of 54–55, 61–62, 151; tactics of, 13–14, 20, 32–33, 153; techniques of, 44, 146–54, 155–56; third-party roles in, 13–14, 40–41, 108–109. *See also* Trieste negotiations
Negotiators: freedom of, 33–34, 54, 55, 147–48; selection of, 25–26, 47, 144, 147–48
Nitze, Paul, 121–22

Parri, Feruccio, 93
Pella, Giuseppe, 57, 61, 68, 83, 138, 152
phases of Trieste negotiations: phase one (United States, Great Britain, Yugoslavia), 14–16, 26–29, 33, 48–52, 97–101; phase two (United States, Great Britain, Italy), 17–20, 28–31, 61–63, 114–19
Piccioni, Attilio, 103, 111, 153
Piran, 16, 27, 99
Pirano. *See* Piran
politics. *See* domestic politics; international politics
Popović, Koča, 91, 95
Popović, Vladimir, 130

press, role in Trieste negotiations, 56, 93–94, 121. *See also* leaks
prestige, role in Trieste negotiations, 18, 28–29, 62, 99, 103, 116, 133, 135
procedure of negotiations, 39–41, 150–51, 155–56; of the Trieste negotiations, 13–14, 17, 26–27, 39–41, 48–49, 94–95, 108–109, 113–14, 119, 148–51
public opinion, role in Trieste negotiations, 96–97. *See also* domestic politics
publicity, effect on Trieste negotiations, 25, 29, 40, 149. *See also* secrecy
Punta Sottile, 18, 19, 63, 69, 102, 116, 118, 135, 152, 153

Ranković, Aleksandar, 101
"Rhodes formula," 150–51
Riddleberger, James, 24, 37, 134, 139
Rijeka. *See* Fiume
Roosevelt, Franklin D., 6, 86

Scelba, Mario, 38, 57, 61, 68, 103, 111, 112, 138, 152
secrecy: in diplomacy, 121–22; effect on Trieste negotiations of, 25, 29, 32–33, 40, 44, 56–57, 73, 93–94, 120–21, 149–50
settlement. *See* Trieste settlement
Sforza, Carlo, 93
Site, selection of, 33, 47, 94
Soča River. *See* Isonzo River
Soviet Union, 8, 21, 75; negotiating with, 44; relations with Yugoslavia, 10, 12, 36, 42, 60–61, 92–93
Stalin, 12, 60
Stassen, Harold, 137
strategies. *See* negotiating strategies
Šubašić, Ivan, 88
Sulzberger, C. L., 149
Sušak, 99

Tarchiani, Alberto, 117

179

INDEX

Tenki Rtič. *See* Punta Sottile
territory, as a factor in the Trieste dispute, 4–6, 8–10, 15, 50–51
Theodoli, Livio, 123
third parties, 108–109; confidence in, 38, 40–41, 95–96, 109, 115, 122–23; influence of, 69–70, 104, 113–14, 148–49, 150; in the Trieste negotiations, 13–14, 40–41, 47, 49, 54–55, 63–64, 69–70, 95–99, 108–109, 111–16, 146–49, 150; selection of, 13–14, 147–48
Thompson, Llewellyn E., 14, 17, 23–44, 50, 54, 55, 95–96, 108 117, 139, 147–49; diplomatic career, 23–24; freedom to negotiate, 33–34, 54, 147–48; instructions to, 14–15, 26, 33–34, 147–48, 170–74; relations with Harrison, 43, 46, 54–55
timing: of negotiations, 109, 156; of the Trieste negotiations, 32, 38, 42, 45–46, 52–53, 71–73, 104–105, 106–107, 146
Tito, Josip Broz-, 6, 11–12, 19, 35, 85, 88, 92, 103, 118, 137–38, 142–43, 149, 152; wartime meeting with Murphy, 131–32, 134
treaties: Italian peace treaty, 7, 20, 21; Italian-Yugoslav following World War I, 4–5; Memorandum of Understanding, 20, 159–62; Rapallo, 5n; Rome, 5n
Trieste: ethnic composition, 77–80; history of the city, 5, 8–10, 77–82; port, 5, 78–79, 81–82
Trieste dispute: background factors, 5–6, 8–10, 16–17, 80–81; effect of the cold war on, 9–12, 84–86; failures to settle, 5–6, 8–9, 11, 25, 32, 35, 46–47; history, 4–7, 9–12, 46–47, 77–88, 145; political context, 6–7, 9–12, 77, 84–86; in Yugoslav politics, 77–82. *See also* Trieste settlement
Trieste negotiations: conclusion, 18–20, 28, 31, 64–65, 102–103, 118, 133–34, 152; conditions, 14–15, 25–26, 112–13; deadlock in, 18–20, 63–64, 69, 117–19, 133–35, 138–39; demands of Italy in, 18, 29–31, 34–35; demands of Yugoslavia in, 16, 26, 27–28, 35, 50–51, 98–99; highlights, 14–21; mediation in, 47, 49, 63–64, 69–70, 95–98, 103–104, 108–109, 111–14, 150; stages, 14, 33, 39–41, 48–49, 62–63, 69–70, 97–98, 102–103, 114, 122–23, 150–51, 155; techniques used in, 20, 26–27, 52, 114–19, 140–41, 146–54; U.S. aid to Yugoslavia as a factor in, 17, 19, 31–32, 58–60, 64, 91–92, 133–34. *See also* bargaining; climate; concessions; delegations; domestic politics; initiatives; instructions; international politics; issues, negotiating strategies; negotiations; negotiators; prestige; procedure; public opinion; publicity; secrecy; site; territory; third parties; timing
Trieste settlement: formula, 39–40, 43, 74–75, 104, 108; permanence, 20, 51–54, 99–100, 126–27, 140, 157–58; success, 41–42, 52–53, 70–71, 100–101; 120–21, 141, 143, 157–58; terms, 16–20, 27–28, 30–31, 61–62, 90–91, 114, 116–17, 140–41, 157–67
tripartite proposal of March 20, 1948, 9–10, 66, 72, 125
Turkey, entente with Greece and Yugoslavia, 12, 60, 66, 106

United Kingdom. *See* Great Britain
United Nations, 9, 21, 53, 107–108
United States: aid to Yugoslavia, 17, 19, 31–32, 58–60, 91–92, 130, 133–34, 136–38; relations with Great Britain, 43, 46, 55–

United States (*cont.*)
56; third-party role, 13–14, 40–41, 49, 103–104, 113–14, 119–20. *See also* Thompson, Llewellyn E.

Velebit, Vladimir, 14, 15, 27, 36, 50, 54, 65, 74, 76–109; freedom to negotiate, 36; instructions to, 94–95, 96
Venezia Giulia. *See* Julian March region
Vukmanović-Tempo, Svetozar, 136–37, 138
Vyshinsky, Andrei, 21, 107

Western allies. *See* Allies
Wheat. *See* United States, aid to Yugoslavia
Wilson, Woodrow, 5

Yugoslavia, 6, 28–29, 82–84; demands in Trieste negotiations, 16–17, 26–28, 35, 50–51, 98–99; entente with Greece and Turkey, 12, 60, 66, 106; ethnic composition, 77–78; factors in willingness to negotiate on Trieste, 35–36, 52–53, 59–61, 71–73, 89–91, 98, 104–105, 111–12, 156; negotiation with the United States and Great Britain, 14–16, 26–29, 33, 48–52, 97–101; as a nonaligned nation, 42, 106–107, 142–43; relations with the Allies, 7, 10–12, 84–88; relations with the Soviet Union, 10–12, 36, 42, 58, 60–61, 66–67, 105–107, 141–43; Trieste dispute in politics of, 77–82; U.S. aid to, 31–32, 58–60, 91–92, 130, 136–38. *See also* Velebit, Vladimir

Zadar, 81
Zara. *See* Zadar
Zaule, 16, 99
Žavlje. *See* Zaule
zones, of the Free Territory of Trieste, 9–19, 27–30, 34, 47–51 61–63, 66, 72, 95, 99, 102, 109, 116, 125, 146, 156, 159, 169, 173
Zoppi, Vittorio, 93, 117, 138

Library of Congress Cataloging in Publication Data
Main entry under title:
Successful negotiation, Trieste 1954.
　　Includes bibliographical references and index.
　　1. Trieste—Politics and government.　2. Italy—Foreign relations—Yugoslavia.　3. Yugoslavia—Foreign relations—Italy.　4. World War, 1939-1945—Territorial questions—Trieste.　I. Campbell, John Coert, 1911-
DG975.T825S9　　　320.9'45'393092　　　75-2981
ISBN 0-691-05658-7

Printed by Libri Plureos GmbH in Hamburg, Germany